A collection of provocative articles
on leadership and management

by Dr. Balaji Krishnamurthy

Balaji Krishnamurthy
Chairman, Think Shift

Dr. Balaji Krishnamurthy is a veteran corporate executive with more than 30 years of corporate experience, having run 16 different businesses in his career. With a Ph.D. in computer science and a strong technology background, he has run a variety of service and manufacturing based, private and public technology businesses ranging from millions of dollars to a billion dollars. As president and CEO of Planar Systems from 1999 to 2005, he led the company's transformation from a sleepy technology company to a leading player in the flat-panel display market. Even as the technology industry collapsed, annual sales of this Nasdaq high-tech company more than doubled under his watch to $256 million. *TIME* magazine recognized him as one of 25 Global Business Influentials, and national publications, such as *The Wall Street Journal,* have featured Balaji and his innovative concepts as representing a new genre of corporate leadership.

Although Balaji has five advanced degrees from prestigious institutions, his concepts of leadership are shaped from the laboratory of corporate experience rather than the classrooms of academic learning. Yet his academic training has caused him to structure his experience into practical models and tools that he has used and taught throughout his career and now teaches to corporate executives. Currently, as the chairman of Think Shift, Balaji communicates his decades of corporate leadership experience through provocative logic and passionate delivery. Known for his innovative and thought provoking concepts on corporate leadership, Balaji works with CEOs to develop organic leadership through an intentional corporate culture.

About Think Shift

In a world of constant change, organizations will either thrive or become irrelevant based on their ability to create and leverage that change. We help you change from the inside out.

Real change starts inside your organization, with your leadership team and employees. We deliver practical tools and advice to build intentional corporate cultures and engaged workplaces. This is the focus of our consulting team.

Successful companies are changing the way they speak with the outside world – shifting from "marketing" to "mattering." To do this, we help you create brands worth caring about, and we share them with your audiences through touchpoints worth experiencing. This is the specialty of our agency division.

This idea of change from the inside out is the foundation of everything we do at Think Shift. We don't see change as some arduous initiative or an obstacle to overcome; we believe intentional change is a powerful tool for creating opportunities that never existed before. We want to help you find and release the potential in your people, your organization, your brand. Change from the inside out means creating inspiring leaders, engaged employees and truly connected customers.

Contents

Introduction

As young preteen boys, my brother and I would often fight.
We had strict rules in the house that forbade physical violence.
But we would argue incessantly.

Often the argument would escalate and one of us would run to our father
to arbitrate. My father had a simple practice, very clever in retrospect. The
moment an issue was brought to his attention, an appeal had been filed with
the court and a court date would be duly set – usually 24 hours hence. Rules
of the court demanded that the contesting parties could not discuss with each
other the contested matter. They may only do so in the presence of the judge,
my father, at the appointed time. Needless to say, the matter not only became
irrelevant, it was totally forgotten 24 hours later. But, on the rare occasion that
one of us did bring up the issue and demand a hearing in the court, my father
would ceremoniously conduct the proceedings. A wooden stool was turned
upside down to serve as a witness stand, inside which each of us would stand.
He would interrogate us on the issue. Rules of the court had emerged over time.
The logic of law and rationale of the rules were carefully explained to us by the
court. The proceedings were intended to be as much of a teaching/learning
experience for the young boys as it was arbitration. Needless to say, both my
brother and I grew up to become good debaters.

I learned through that process that there are two sides to every issue. It now
bothers me when somebody paints a lopsided picture of an issue. So much so
that I want to argue the other side, independent of my personal opinion on the
matter. My wife hates it when I don't agree with her account of something she
read in the newspaper during our Sunday morning coffee time. Although my
wife and I are very aligned on our political and social views, I am apt to take
the other point of view just to have a more balanced discussion. Married to her
for more than 35 years, I am learning to avoid those situations.

Likewise, I have a strong dislike for motherhood and apple pie – statements that say nothing new and with which few would disagree. "If you want growth, focus on sales," says one such motherhood. "Your people are your most valuable asset," says another. Statements like these make me discount the source. I prefer statements that are a bit more controversial. I recently heard the quote, "Your people are not your most important asset, some of your people are." Although it conveys the message of the earlier motherhood statement, it says it with an edge. Essentially, it says not all of your people are your most valuable asset; just a few of them are. Even if you do not agree with it, you must concede that it provokes thought. Likewise, focusing on sales for growth is a motherhood statement. Consider this alternative: You are better off with a superior sales channel and a mediocre product than a mediocre channel and a superior product. Again, independent of your agreement with the position, this latter statement is not motherhood and apple pie.

Jack Welch, long-time CEO of General Electric, used to promote a concept that I call the Jack Welch formula. He stated that organizations needed to have energy, emotion and edge. Energy is not a new requirement. Emotion was simply an "E" word for passion, also a common requirement. Where Welch distinguished himself is in the requirement of edge. What is edge? Edge is the idea that the concept has been taken to a point where there is some controversy. The proposal must push the envelope to a point where some think it might break. The thought must reach the edge of the cliff beyond which it will self-destruct. If you don't have edge, Welch would argue, you are simply mediocre. I believe creating controversy creates edge.

In 2007, I started writing a newsletter called *Food for Thought*. My intent was to share provocative ideas that might be controversial. I wanted to make sure I provided both sides of an issue. It was intended to be a bite-sized idea that could be captured in an email and might be of interest to corporate executives. It went to about a hundred executives. I never imagined that it would turn into a monthly mailing that would last almost a decade and go to more than 5,000 recipients. No doubt, coming up with a bite-sized, provocative and controversial idea to share every month has not been without its challenges. But it also sparked many new ideas. I cannot say I succeeded to be provocative with all of them. But I did get there with some of them. With more than 85 ideas discussed over that time period, I thought it would be useful to compile them into a collection.

What was common to the ideas? Was there a theme? Was there a pattern? Yes and no. Should I create a simple collection of the ideas? Should the collection be organized? Should it be presented chronologically to preserve the original flow of thought? Or should it be grouped and ordered? Should the pieces be re-written for present context? And these were only the starting questions. I chose to leave the articles exactly as originally written, except for minor editing. But I decided to group them into related topics. A consequence of that decision is that there are many articles that refer to events of their time. Although they are now events of the past, the topic remains germane and relevant. There are a lot of articles on compensation and performance management, and there is a large collection of miscellaneous items. Of note is the group on a provocative holiday tradition. I introduce the topic at the beginning of that chapter.

The articles were originally written under the company name LogiStyle. In 2014, we merged with a Canadian company to form our current company called Think Shift. The subsequent articles are written under that name. So some articles refer to our company as LogiStyle and some refer to it as Think Shift.

The underlying theme of all of the articles is to be provocative and controversial. I hope you find them so.

Personal Development

When I started LogiStyle, I hired new college graduates to assist me in marketing our workshops.

They were eager to learn the business material being taught in the workshops. They interacted with CEOs and other executives who attended the workshops. There were lots of opportunities for me to teach them business lessons in the office. They were empowered to run the geographic territory assigned to them like a mini business. However, in a few years they had learned all they were going to learn at LogiStyle. The company was too small for them to advance to any new position. So we had a policy that every employee would leave in about three years.

I would make this policy clear at the outset during hiring. I would discuss their progression toward this goal at each monthly one-on-one meeting. Initially, the discussions would start with an exploration of what they might want to do, the kind of companies they might want to work for, the kind of jobs they might want to pursue, etc. Slowly, the conversation would move to specific companies and any specific jobs they might have. The employee would keep me in the loop as they pursued opportunities. I would coach them before they went to an interview. When they finally landed a job, we would work together to plan the transition. And I would hire another individual and start all over again.

I got a lot of pleasure in growing young people during the formative portion of their business careers. Executives have a stewardship responsibility to develop their people. You must leave behind a richer set of assets – human capital assets – at the end of the year than you had at the beginning of the year. Ask yourself whether every employee in your company is richer for the experiences at the end of the year than they were at the beginning of the year. That is a stewardship responsibility we have.

This chapter is about personal development. Some of the articles refer to my practice at LogiStyle.

To Attract Young Talent, Think Young

June 2009

There's been a lot of talk about how young college graduates seem to have a very different notion of a successful work life than older generations had in their youth. Even highly accomplished graduates, coming out of prestigious schools, choose such an eclectic mix of disciplines that the high achievers of past generations would label them as "lost in life." And can we blame them? The excesses and debacles of corporate America have only made young people wearier of a carefully planned career. But attracting young talent with fresh new ideas is critical to the health of our businesses. So how do modern corporations attract talent from a generation of skeptics? I have an idea.

Abandon the traditional approach of finding candidates to fill open positions and adopt a new approach of creating attractive positions to suit good candidates. In other words, do away with the notion of established jobs with prescribed titles and assigned roles and responsibilities. Instead, create a new dynamic by dividing up the work that needs to be done among currently available talent. Better yet, when new talent becomes available, design roles and responsibilities that would be most suitable and attractive for that individual.

We should be looking to attract good people, not looking to fill open positions.

Just as the previous generation was fixated on the notion of lifetime employment and perplexed by baby boomers who would switch jobs multiple times through their careers, let's not become fixated on the younger generation sticking to a specific, traditional career path. Young people crave variety and are more likely to pursue many interests at once. And that craving goes beyond hobbies, carrying over into their educations and lifestyles too. The best corporations will find ways to accommodate that desire and get the best out of young people's curiosity and diversity.

Coaching Through Advocacy

January 2013

This month's topic is inspired by some polarizing political debates underway in the U.S., but the topic itself is not political.

Even though many of my foreign readers might have little interest in U.S. politics, they no doubt are aware of these issues. Over the last few months in the U.S., we've seen polarizing debates leading up to the presidential elections in November, stalemate conversations leading up to the fiscal cliff in December and a horrific tragedy in Sandy Hook that has rekindled an ideological conversation on gun control. What these conversations have in common is that many people have entrenched positions. They don't just believe they're right, they know they're right.

These conversations remind me of many business issues I have faced in my career – conversations where technically competent individuals have strongly held views, but it's up to the less technically competent executive or CEO to make the call.

The technical nature of the issue might be understanding a piece of machinery that needs to be purchased, a vendor that needs to be selected or a financial issue that requires technical understanding. With many of these business issues, there are entrenched positions with ardent supporters. And in most cases, the CEO is the least technically competent. Yet the CEO has to make the call.

There's a tool called Coaching Through Advocacy that CEOs (or the decision-making executives) can use in these situations.

The idea of this tool is to force the ardent advocate to live in the other world. When they do, they find the other world is not as dark as they once thought it was. The CEO identifies an ardent supporter from each side who is outspoken and articulate. Let's call these individuals Alice and Bob. Alice is tasked with making a 10-minute speech in front of a large audience, advocating Bob's position with gusto and never straying from it.

Likewise, Bob is tasked with making a 10-minute speech advocating Alice's position. The CEO invites everyone concerned to the ceremony. And in this case, ceremony demands that the CEO occupies a central seat flanked on either side by all the influencers of the decision. Note: Do NOT physically divide the influencers by their positions. All other invitees, including all of the people that are affected by the decision, are asked to sit and act as observers. The CEO then explains the tasks assigned to Alice and Bob and lays out the ground rules of interaction:

- Alice and Bob speak for 10 minutes, advocating the side assigned to each, and during those 10 minutes no questions will be entertained.

- After the 20 minutes, the panel of influencers may ask Alice and Bob questions. During this period, Alice and Bob must continue to play the roles assigned to them.

- At the end of the questioning, Alice and Bob are relieved of their roles and may join the influencers in a group conversation.

What are the advantages of this process?

First of all, Alice and Bob are forced to not only understand the other person's point of view but to communicate it to their supporters, who might be more willing to consider the other side. During the question-and-answer period, the other influencers can force Alice and Bob to expand on the arguments they might have conveniently omitted. All of this makes everybody more comfortable with imagining a world in which their feared choice ends up winning. And they realize that world is not so bad after all. In fact, they begin to appreciate some of the good things about that world. That feared world becomes more palatable. Most importantly, those who are on the fence begin to form an opinion. Their voices are often the most reasoned voices for the CEO to hear.

The advantage of a business environment – compared to the political environment of Washington – is that the CEO can make a unilateral decision.

However, it's important that the CEO understands and appreciates the nuanced technical issues. Coaching Through Advocacy provides a process to do just that. In a democratic environment, this process might not work. But even there, imagine if the speaker of the house and the senate majority leader – John Boehner and Harry Reid – each had to give a nationally televised speech for 10 minutes arguing the other side! That would be a riot.

Small Companies Must Turnover Good People

April 2011

At LogiStyle, I have typically hired recent college graduates, offering them education in corporate leadership and promising them opportunities to interact with CEOs from a broad range of industries.

They're unlikely to find these opportunities in other jobs, and we have been lucky enough to attract talented employees who rise to the challenge. Many of you have had an opportunity to interact with our team, but there are limitations to their jobs. If you asked me what advancement opportunities they have at LogiStyle, I'd say there aren't any! It's just not reasonable to expect one of them to supplement or replace me and deliver workshops on leadership. So we make this clear to them right from the time we hire them. We tell them that this is a great opportunity for a recent college graduate for about three years. After that, they should plan on moving on to the next step in their career. Does that pose a burden on LogiStyle? You bet it does! But what is the alternative? Should we hire someone who's content to do this job for 20 years? What kind of employee would we get?

LogiStyle is a tiny company. Small companies that might be larger than LogiStyle have this problem too. In any company with a pyramid-like hierarchy, there are few opportunities at the top. In a small company, opportunities for talented and aspiring employees are rare and often limited – at LogiStyle, they're nonexistent! You're better off recognizing and acknowledging this. You can then work with the employee to develop an appropriate career plan inside or outside of your company.

There is a positive correlation between high performers and people with high aspirations. Good employees are going to want bigger challenges and larger responsibilities. When your small company has limited opportunities, you're better off letting them move on or even helping them find that next opportunity at another company. If you work with them, they will work with you to make the transition smooth for both of you. What is the alternative? Would you want to hire people who are content doing the same job every day for decades? You'll fall prey to *The Gallery Owner's Dilemma*! (See page 98.)

Succession Planning Through Musical Chairs

May 2007

Succession planning is usually an activity centered on **key positions** in a company. But at a recent meeting with corporate executives, we discussed succession planning as centered on **key individuals** in a company and worked through an interesting experiment.

Imagine the following memo, written by the CEO of a mid-sized company with a few thousand employees and addressed to 200 mid-level managers.

Dear Fellow Managers,

As you know, I am a firm believer in providing development and growth opportunities for our employees and, at the same time, ensuring that the company has the leadership personnel it needs to ensure succession plans for its key positions. In support of these goals, I am asking all of our managers to undertake the following exercise in earnest.

I would like each of you to identify two or three other positions in the company that you feel you're qualified for and would be interested in, should the position become available. Approach the managers of those positions and go through a formal interview, seeking their input on your readiness to fill that position. I would hope that, in the process, you would hear their candid assessment of any specific deficiencies in your skills and competencies, and, in return, you would offer them your views on how you might approach the duties of that job from your own unique perspective. This exercise is not intended to result in an offer of a new assignment, but merely an exploration of each other's mutual interest.

I have asked our human resources department to create a minimal process to track the positions you are interested in and the feedback of the interviewing managers. You should view this as a proactive career-planning step on your part. For the company, this data becomes a starting point when vacancies arise at key positions. My intent is merely to cause both you and the company to do this proactively before the actual need arises. My personal focus would be on positions in the company that are not coveted by anyone, and on specific individuals that do not seem to have a clear growth opportunity.

I hope you will undertake this exercise with enthusiasm, reaching for positions you aspire to and causing conversations that reveal fresh and novel perspectives. Thank you for adding this to your full plate of daily duties.

Happy exploring.

Your CEO

How do you think the recipient managers would react?

As the news of this memo spread throughout the company, what would be the reaction? What would the CEO and the company learn from this experiment? Would any CEO actually issue such a memo?

Well, one company has implemented this process and two more are currently exploring it. The company that did implement it learned interesting lessons. First of all, as you might expect, there was immediate anxiety and concern when the memo went out. "The CEO is looking to eliminate certain positions and people," the rumor mill asserted. But as the process unfolded, it wasn't the people looking for positions that felt at risk but rather the incumbents of those positions.

The most surprising part was the amount of energy it created within the organization as new ideas for old activities began to circulate. By the end of the process, nearly the entire management team shared the same enthusiasm and each participant was eager to find his or her next assignment – I'm not kidding! Best of all, most of the movement within the company was horizontal with people moving to positions that senior management would never have imagined – proof that this exercise allows people to broaden their horizons. Succession planning had changed. It wasn't driven from the top down; it was energized from the bottom up.

Is It Time to Prepare the Envelopes?

October 2007

There's an old corporate joke about a departing manager leaving behind three numbered envelopes in their desk drawer. The departing manager advises the new incoming manager to open one of the envelopes for advice when faced with a difficult management problem. Within a couple of days, the new manager resorts to the first envelope, which reads, "Blame it on the last guy." Empowered to blame all things wrong on the last guy, the new manager makes numerous changes but soon finds it necessary to open the second envelope. "Reorganize," the envelope advises. With a reorganized management team, the company moves along merrily for a few years. One day, while pondering a difficult management problem, the now mature manager recalls the long forgotten third envelope tucked away in the desk drawer and eagerly seeks its advice: "Prepare three envelopes."

Few people have the same level of energy and enthusiasm after three years in their job as they did in their first three days.

When you start a new job, you usually walk into it with a modest set of assets but without any liabilities. Your assets consist of all your previous education and experiences that makes you acceptably qualified for doing the job. And your assets grow as you grow in that role. This growth in assets is dramatic in the initial months on the job but slows down over time and tends to start petering out in just a few years.

Pretty soon, you find yourself having used up your entire bag of tricks and short on new ideas to face the daily challenges of the job. In contrast to the growth of your assets, your liabilities on the job start out practically at zero. You have no baggage. You start with a clean slate, but eventually you make mistakes. You make a wrong decision, you make some wrong hires, you enter some wrong markets or you take a public stance that turns out to be wrong. In most of these cases, people around you realize the error of your ways before you do. These wrong moves become your liabilities. And the liabilities continue to grow, slowly but incessantly. Soon enough – say, after a few years – your assets have petered out, and your liabilities just keep on growing. It's time to prepare those envelopes.

Even though your assets are not growing, or not growing rapidly, you might still have a strong base of assets to do the job and do it well. So why should you leave the job? The problem is that your liabilities continue to grow, deteriorating your net contribution. So how could you shed yourself of those liabilities? If you move to a new job, you could leave your baggage behind. That's why the new guy comes with no baggage. They left it at the curbside! But what if you were the CEO? Would you have to go to a new company? Would it be fair to your current company? Would it be fair to you? What if you were the owner or a major shareholder? You couldn't just up and leave!

How do you, a CEO with an established tenure, shed your baggage? It's actually quite simple. Declare yourself as the new guy.

Do this ceremoniously and with fanfare. Do this when it would be most convenient to make a change at the top. When a CEO tried this method, he invited the chairman of the board to declare to the management team, at the annual kickoff of their fiscal year, that the board had decided to bring in a new CEO. You might even try refreshing your style to go with your fresh start, maybe dressing more casually, changing your hairstyle or color or any other visible change to represent your transformation.

Now that you've been declared the new guy, keep introducing yourself at meetings and events, and feel free to blame all things wrong on the last guy. Do this purposely and with a straight face. Make those changes that you were always opposed to but others advocated. Give your management team a fresh new performance appraisal and blame any inconsistencies on the last guy. Be open to a totally different organizational structure. At meetings and discussions, play dumb about the last guy's rationale for past actions and have others explain to you what the last guy was thinking. All of this empowers you to shed your baggage while empowering the organization to relieve you of it.

The basic idea here is not new.

Gordon Moore and Andy Grove are known to have asked themselves, "What would a new guy do?" while pondering over Intel's memory business. Jack

Welch is known to have reinvented himself every six years or so with a passion for a new concept, which he drove across General Electric. This idea of declaring yourself as the new guy is merely a dramatic way of implementing the basic concepts that leaders like Moore, Grove and Welch found easy to embrace.

Excitement of the New and Unknown

February 2013

This month's article is, in part, a farewell to Gwen Hickmond, a look forward at the new person we will be hiring to replace Gwen, and a reiteration of a leadership tool called Personal Assets and Liabilities.

Many of you know Gwen Hickmond, who was with LogiStyle for two and a half years. You might have met her at one of our workshops or spoken to her on the phone. She has moved on to the next rung in her career, a wonderful marketing opportunity with JBA Consulting Engineers. With this *Food for Thought* article, we celebrate her move and wish her success. Our excitement and joy probably needs explanation. Why is an employer happy to see their employee move on to the next job?

At LogiStyle, we hire recent college graduates, usually with little or no work experience, offer them a great opportunity to learn about marketing, event planning and leadership, and give them an opportunity to interact with accomplished corporate executives and CEOs at our workshops. While it is a great job for a recent college graduate, there is little growth opportunity within our small company. So we tell them at the time of hiring that this job is good for about three years. They should use it as a stepping stone for their next career move. We help them through that process by forcing the conversation at each of their monthly, one-on-one meetings with me. From day one on the job, they are required to articulate their career interests, do research on where and how they could fulfill those aspirations, take active steps to explore those possibilities and, in two to three years, settle on the right opportunity and move forward. In our short history of six years, Stefanie Call, Emily Meath and Courtney Brinkhoff have moved on. Now it is Gwen Hickmond's turn.

Interestingly enough, Gwen was recruited by one of our clients. Dwayne Miller, CEO of JBA Consulting Engineers, had met Gwen and spent three days with her at one of our L³ workshops, where Gwen was responsible for the entire event – the selection of the location, the negotiation with the hotel to draft a contract, the marketing of the event, registration of participants, all of the arrangements for the event and orchestration of the event on-site. When

Dwayne heard of our transition policy, he asked us if he could consider her for a position in his company. Then, in the most professional way, he handed over the opportunity to one of his managers who had an open position and let that manager consider Gwen on his own terms.

Of course, we celebrate Gwen's transition with mixed emotions. Gwen contributed greatly to LogiStyle. She was very comfortable here. The staff referred to her as the boss, since I was always traveling and seldom in the office. But imagine Gwen's excitement – and discomfort – this week, starting a new job. Everything is new and different. Nothing is familiar. A great opportunity in front of her. How she presents herself, deals with situations, interacts with people, etc. in the next six months will shape her capacity to influence and contribute in this new position. She is probably excited and she is probably nervous. There is excitement in the new and unknown. There is power in that excitement.

Ask yourself how many of your employees have that excitement they had in their first six months. Chances are you are listing the employees that joined in the last six months. What are you doing to maintain that excitement? What are you doing to keep them from getting comfortable? Is being comfortable in a job a good thing? Or does it lead to complacency and stagnation? Would you rather have somebody still growing into the job or would you prefer somebody who already knows everything about the job? In which situation is more value being created for the employer and the employee, both individually and collectively? How comfortable are your employees?

We have maintained that when an employee leaves a company and returns after a few years, the success of that re-hire is likely to be less than if you had made a brand new hire. Of course, there are exceptions to this rule. One of the drawbacks of a returning hire is that they don't have that same sense of excitement. They are likely to be more comfortable than a brand new hire. You want your new employee to have that sense of excitement and discomfort.

We will soon be hiring a new employee to replace Gwen. We are looking forward to the excitement, ideas, enthusiasm and untainted perspective that this new person will bring us. Is that worth the cost of training the new person into the job? Absolutely!

Leadership

I define leadership as the product of leverage and legacy. Leaders influence people. They influence people to think differently. They influence people to act differently. They influence people to behave differently. The number of people the leader influences represents the leverage. The length of time over which the influence lasts represents the legacy. Great leaders have high leverage and long legacy.

I believe that leadership cannot be taught, learned or imitated; it must be developed. Each of us is our own unique kind of leader; we must find that style of leadership. As Oscar Wilde aptly put it, "Be yourself; everybody else is taken!" The idea of learning or teaching leadership suggests that somebody already knows it. In contrast, the idea of developing leadership suggests that it has to be created. When you switch your thinking of leadership from one of learning to one of developing, you undertake a personal responsibility for creating your own unique style of leadership.

The articles in this chapter try to emphasize that there is no right or wrong, good or bad. Just a different style for each of us. Yet, knowing what your natural style is and what style might work best in a given situation allows you to be intentional about the style you wish to use.

Are You Specific or Diffuse?

February 2014

Different people tend to speak with different levels of specificity. Over this past Super Bowl weekend, somebody commented, "I like watching the Super Bowl for its commercials." This is a statement of personal preference with some broad judgment intended. It's unlikely that somebody would disagree with this judgment since it's stated as a personal preference. But that individual could have said, "Some of the Super Bowl commercials are really funny," or "Super Bowl commercials are really well done." Each of these expressions takes a position a listener could easily disagree with. Some people speak with specificity and some people speak in more diffuse terms.

Although it depends on the situation and the subject matter, we all have a tendency to be more specific or more diffuse compared to those around us.

For example, somebody taking a sip of coffee poured from a fresh pot and finding it lukewarm might comment, "You know, coffee is best when served at 180 degrees Farenheit." This is a very specific statement, so specific it practically forces listeners to decide whether they agree or not. A listener might not question the position, but they will agree or disagree either implicitly or explicitly. People who are **"specific"** either expect that others will agree with them or are usually less concerned with disagreement. Their goal is to establish a very clear position, and they are often happy to take on opposing points of view. They will often express their opinions as statements of truth. People who are specific aren't ones to shy away from controversy or disagreement.

However, in the example of the lukewarm coffee, the coffee enthusiast could have said, "You know, coffee is best when it's served rather hot." Notwithstanding the iced-coffee fans, it's hard to disagree with that statement. It's diffuse enough to allow for people with a variety of opinions to find some common ground in it. People who are **"diffuse"** speak with less specificity so that all listeners can find some overlap in their position. They are more interested in finding common ground and then narrowing the common ground as far as possible, than finding the contrast between their position and the other person's. When they want to be specific, they'll often express it as their opinion.

People who are diffuse tend to shy away from controversy and disagreement.

Is one better than the other?

Should we label ourselves and others as specific or diffuse? Do we always speak in one way or the other? Clearly, the answer is "no" to all those questions. However, if you observe yourself, you will find that you have a tendency to be more one type than the other. By becoming self-aware of your natural tendency, you can be more intentional about how you speak in particular situations and with particular audiences.

Some audiences – accountants, lawyers and engineers come to mind (sorry for the stereotyping) – tend to be specific in their communication and might find overly diffuse conversations full of platitudes and lacking in substance. On the other hand, other audiences – artists, salespeople and politicians come to mind (again, my apologies) – tend to be diffuse in their communication and might find overly specific conversations obnoxious and opinionated. By being aware of your audience, you can balance your needs and theirs to determine how specific or diffuse you should be in that situation.

I close with a self-referential question: Is this article specific or diffuse? How could this article have been written to be more specific or more diffuse?

Specific Versus Diffuse

May 2015

Last month, David Baker, our CEO, wrote a provocative article challenging axioms – statements we believe to be self-evident truths. I want to thank David for filling in during my vacation. I also want to use him as an example of how to intentionally use both specific and diffuse forms of communication effectively.

A year ago, I noted that some people are specific in their communication, intentionally bringing forth clarity of thought, and others are more diffuse, intentionally bringing forth commonality of thought.

Both styles have value, and the value is enhanced if you're intentional about your natural style and the style that's appropriate for your audience. While my natural style is specific, David Baker is able to use either style based on what is appropriate for the audience. Let me provide two examples of David's writing to illustrate this point.

In last month's *Food for Thought,* David wanted to respect the provocative nature of these articles.

To be provocative and controversial, you need to be specific in establishing your point of view and contrasting it with alternative points of view.

In analyzing the axiom, "If you are going to bring me a problem, make sure you bring with it a solution," David points out that the traditional view contrasts an employee who is building with an employee who is throwing rocks. Having been specific in that contrast, he then switches his position, providing convincing arguments as to why you should encourage employees to raise issues for which they have no solution. His style of specific communication is very effective.

A couple decades ago, I learned an interesting lesson. Trained as an engineer, with a background in math and a passion for logic, I have always been specific in my communication. But while listening to my VP of marketing tell our sales force about a new series of products we were introducing, I learned that using **diffuse communication might achieve your results better than being specific.** He drew a graph, labeled the x-axis with old products and new products, talked about how the old products had floundered, spoke about the amazing value of the new products and drew a sweeping line that zigzagged from the bottom left to the top right, proclaiming that our new products were going to take our business to new heights.

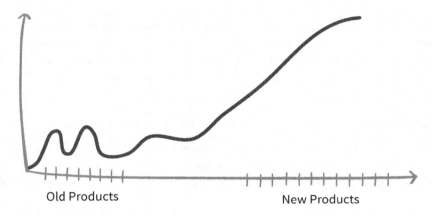

Old Products   New Products

Questions came to my mind: *What was the x-axis? Products? How were they arranged? By introduction date? What was the y-axis? Units? Dollars? Was this a cumulative graph? If so, how did the graph go down with the current products?* I was trying to figure it all out. Meanwhile, our sales force had heard the rallying cry. They were pumped. They cheered! Hadn't my marketing VP accomplished his goal? Does it matter that the graph didn't make any sense? Being diffuse might have been the best way to communicate to that audience at that moment!

Let's come back to David Baker. In his monthly blog, David wrote an interesting post titled *What is Normal?* He pointed out that, while most people try to fit in and be normal, it is the outliers that get noticed. To make his point he drew this picture.

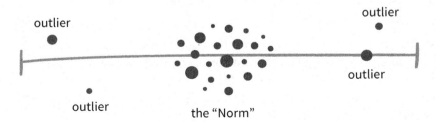

outlier

outlier

outlier

outlier

the "Norm"

Of course, I had a plethora of questions: *What does the line mean? What do circles represent on the left side versus the right side? How about circles above and below? Are circles above the line better than those below or different in some other way? And what do the size of the circles mean? Are bigger circles better?* Yet in spite of all my questions, I understood what he was saying in the article. The picture communicated it. **Was he being diffuse? Absolutely! Was he effective in his communication? Superbly!** In a blog, where typically the intent is to connect with people rather than provoke them, diffuse communication allows each reader to interpret the information and potentially find common ground with the writer.

It's important to understand both specific and diffuse communication.

Each has its value. Each is more effective in different circumstances. Each of us has a preference in our own individual style. Yet we owe it to ourselves to use the right style for the right situation.

On this topic, my good friend and colleague Glenn Mangurian pointed out that **the appropriate style not only depends on the circumstance, but the speaker-listener chemistry as well.** Glenn and I developed the following model for what might happen based on whether the speaker and the listener are specific or diffuse:

- When *the speaker and listener are both specific,* they are likely to assert and evaluate. On the positive side, they might find clear agreement or disagreement and extend their thought process. But the same conversation could turn into a debate or argument, with each trying to prove that they are right.

- When *the speaker is specific and the listener is diffuse,* they are likely to assert and consider. The listener respects the speaker's point of view and learns. But the speaker could also be viewed as being arrogant and opinionated, with the listener agreeing in pretense.

- When *the speaker is diffuse and the listener is specific,* they are likely to explore but evaluate. The listener is likely to ask for clarification and agree or offer a different point of view. Alternatively, the conversation could turn into an argument where the listener browbeats the speaker for specificity that the speaker either does not have or is not willing to offer.

- When *the speaker and the listener are both diffuse,* the conversation is likely to explore and agree. Both the speaker and listener could become innovative and the conversation could become generative. But the conversation could just as easily meander without reaching a conclusion, with both the speaker and the listener agreeing without really understanding.

		Listener	
		Diffuse	**Specific**
Speaker	**Specific**	Assert & Consider	Assert & Evaluate
	Diffuse	Explore & Agree	Explore & Evaluate

In each case, conversation can take on a positive tone and create value, or it can take on a negative tone and destroy value.

It's important that we acknowledge the natural tendencies of the speaker and listener and intentionally drive the conversation toward positive, value-creating outcomes.

I started the article thanking David for filling in last month. I want to applaud him for his ability to deftly switch modes when appropriate. I'd also like to thank him for helping me illustrate the value of being intentionally specific or diffuse. You really should read his monthly blog at www.shiftinthinking.com.

Are You a Linear or Non-Linear Thinker?

March 2014

Have you ever heard somebody say that so-and-so is a "linear thinker"? Or somebody might proudly say, "I am a non-linear thinker." What do they mean?

The word "linear" comes from the root "line."

The thoughts of a linear thinker tend to form a line (i.e. one thought leads to the next, then to the next, and so on). In calling someone a linear thinker, we assume that their thought process is easy to understand and that the conclusions seem logically sound. We do this with an underlying judgment that their conclusions are usually not that profound. In contrast, a non-linear thinker tends to have a myriad of unrelated thoughts that somehow interrelate. These thoughts lead to conclusions that might otherwise not have been evident. We tend to think the non-linear thinker's conclusions are more profound and insightful – hence, the pride in claiming yourself to be a non-linear thinker.

Common stereotypes often make scientists, accountants and analytical types out to be linear thinkers, while artists, designers and creative types tend to be labeled as non-linear thinkers.

Is that generally true? Is introducing a sampling of non-linear thinkers into a staff of linear thinkers helpful in engendering creativity? Can linear and non-linear thinkers coexist and work together? More importantly, can they communicate effectively with each other?

Before I answer those questions, let us look at linear and non-linear thinkers from a less linear perspective. See what I did there?

Consider the unsolved "P versus NP" question from the field of computer science. It is one of the Millennium Prize Problems posed by the Clay Mathematics Institute and it asks: Is it harder for computers to find the solution to a problem than to verify that a found solution actually works? It is generally believed that finding the solution is significantly more difficult than verifying a solution. For example, can you pull together a select group of employees in your company whose balances in their company 401(K) account averages to precisely $100,000? Finding the right set of employees might be difficult. But once found, demonstrating that their account balances averages to $100,000 is relatively easy. It's generally believed that you need creativity of thought for the search but, once the solution is found, you need clarity of thought for its communication.

Let's go back to linear and non-linear thinkers.

Do we sometimes confuse the thinking process with the communication process? Do we sometimes call people non-linear thinkers if they can't articulate their thoughts clearly? Just because their communication is all over the place doesn't mean that they have derived benefit from being disorganized in their thinking. They might just be haphazard thinkers. Likewise, do we confuse organized thinkers with linear thinkers? Even if the search for the thought requires non-linear thinking, one needs to be able to articulate it clearly. I believe that a lack of clarity in communicating one's thought is often a sign that one doesn't fully understand the thought.

I also believe a non-linear organized thinker is ideal. These people can find connections between seemingly unrelated thoughts, then present it to you in a simple, clear way. If you can get these people into your team, they will engender creativity.

How can you instill non-linear, organized thinking? Here is one possible technique:

We are all familiar with the concept of brainstorming. A group of people generates ideas, all of which are recorded and none of which are judged. When the ideas run out, they look at the whole list. The next time you reach this stage, use the technique of **Affinity Mapping** to group the ideas into categories that make sense. Write each idea on a sticky note, paste all the sticky notes on a wall and let the people move the sticky notes around to group related thoughts together. Again, like in the brainstorming phase, nobody has to justify why they moved one sticky note next to another. In fact, a sticky note might bounce back and forth, like a yo-yo, between two groups of notes. When this part of the process reaches a natural end, have the group or one participant create a total story of what all the groups say. You have promoted non-linear thinking with organized communication.

Affinity Mapping is one of the tools in our tool chest. The concept of leadership tools and the amassing of a large tool chest are critical to becoming an intentional leader. And, as you know, that's what I'm all about: developing intentional leaders.

Do You Focus on the Income Statement or the Balance Sheet?

April 2010

When CEOs with far too much on their plates are faced with either hiring a general manager to take over one of their divisions or hiring a director of organizational development to take care of growing their employees, they usually opt for the latter. "After all," they argue, "being in direct control of the division – its customers, its products and its profits – will have an immediate impact on this year's financial performance."

A good way to examine where a CEO should focus their time is to ask whether the CEO is making an Income Statement Contribution or a Balance Sheet Contribution.

Notice that some balance sheet contributions, like personal development, create intangible assets, not just financial assets. Income statement contributions are easy to recognize: they can usually be well defined, quantified and measured, and have a more immediate impact (i.e. this period or this year). And their impact is a one-time event. In contrast, balance sheet contributions are often intangible, like establishing a new enterprise resource planning system, which is usually more difficult to quantify and measure. And the resulting asset often pays off in perpetuity, or at least for a long, long time.

As a rule of thumb, CEOs should focus more of their time on developing balance sheet assets and be more willing to delegate income statement responsibility to their executives.

The long-term value of balance sheet assets is often greater than the one-time effect of income statement accomplishments. Besides, it's easier to hold your executives responsible for delivering on income statement commitments than to ensure they've created intangible balance sheet assets.

In fact, this philosophy can be used to analyze any annual performance plan, prepared at the outset of the year. What line items in your performance plan provide a one-time income statement contribution for this year? What line items develop balance sheet assets that pay in perpetuity? A balanced performance plan has a good mix of both. Most executives are so focused on delivering this year's results that their performance plan is lopsided in favor of income statement contributions. It's time to stop neglecting the balance sheet.

The Power of Complementation

September 2013

Over the last few months, I've had the chance to reconnect with colleagues from both my present and my past. During these conversations, I noticed these colleagues share an attribute that has significantly benefited me over the years. This article is a personal reflection on the power of complementation, the importance of surrounding yourself with people who complement you.

Complement (as opposed to compliment) is derived from the word complete. It brings to mind the idea of "fitting together" or "filling out the other half."

A person complements you if the two of you have enough similarities to connect and enough differences to make the whole more than the sum of its parts. I've been fortunate enough to have had a number of colleagues complement me over the years. I want to share with you some of the working relationships I've had with my colleagues and offer suggestions about how you could be intentional in using the power of complementation.

Glenn Mangurian is a renowned speaker and thinker on leadership and management. He and I are very much alike. Yet we could not be further apart.

We both have a passion for leadership, a belief in the power of intentionality and authenticity and a desire to create leaders within organizations. But we go about it in two very different ways. I prefer to be non-prescriptive and provocative; he prefers to understand, agree and extend. I prefer to poke holes in others' ideas with the intent to create something better; he prefers to compliment and complement with the same intent: to create something better. We are both equally passionate but in our own ways. He is as calm and encouraging as I am energetic and excited. We have enough similarities to connect and enough differences to make a greater whole. We've also had great fun working together.

Then there was "the trifecta" at Planar, where I was the CEO for many years.

In the Balaji, Steve Buhaly, Carolyn McKnight trifecta, each pair of us had something in common and we complemented the third. Steve and I were rational, logical thinkers; Carolyn and I dreamed and embraced unusual ideas; and Carolyn and Steve were attuned to the emotions of people and organizations. Together, we made a great team. Complementation is not just about filling out the other half. It's also about how you connect to make a seamless fit.

Then there are the famous examples:

Steve Jobs and Tim Cook at Apple: Jobs, the dreamer, and Cook, the guy who executed the dream. Marie and Pierre Curie: Marie, understanding the potential value of their technical work, and Pierre, understanding how the university and the technical systems of France worked to get things done.

Are you enjoying the power of complementation?

Are you surrounding yourself with the right people? Take a look at yourself and your executive staff. Understand the difference between what's common and what's complementary in your dynamic. Become intentional about using the complementation you have and proactively seek out others who fill in the missing pieces in your organizational puzzle.

Acknowledging that this article isn't as provocative as my usual articles, I'll close with a provocative thought instead. In our Seven Secrets for Successful Leadership workshop, one of the secrets we discuss is "Embrace Controversy; Beware of Consensus." In explaining this concept, I claim that half your staff should disagree with you in most major decisions. Believe it or not, that is the power of complementation.

When Was the Last Time You Publicly Admitted You Were Wrong?

March 2012

This article was inspired by a letter from the Oracle of Omaha, Warren Buffett. In his annual letter to the shareholders of Berkshire Hathaway, Buffett admitted he was wrong – not just wrong, dead wrong! He said, "Last year, I told you that a housing recovery will probably begin within a year or so. I was dead wrong."

How many leaders have the courage to say that they were wrong – that their prediction, their decision, their new hire, their pet project, the business they ventured, the company they bought was the wrong idea? Yet leaders who are willing to publicly admit their errors are, in fact, more revered.

Ask yourself: When was the last time you publicly admitted you were wrong?

Better yet, ask yourself this: What do you hold dear right now that others around you question? The thing that (in their opinion) you refuse to examine objectively. Asking yourself about the present is always more uncomfortable than the academic question of examining the past.

As a CEO, I have made a point to publicly self-assess my performance for the previous year.

People have always asked me, "Don't your shortcomings make you look weak to your employees?"

My response has always been, "Who am I trying to fool? Don't they know my failures already? They probably came to those conclusions before I even realized them!"

As a leader, you need to have the courage of your conviction to take a stance but also the honor and humility to admit when you are wrong. The former is the easy part. Try focusing more on the latter.

Intentionality Versus Authenticity

August 2013

Intentionality is the central message in all of my workshops. If you have ever heard me speak anywhere, you probably heard the word "intentional" used multiple times in multiple forms. When I talk about leadership, I declare that leadership cannot be taught, learned or imitated; it has to be developed and developed intentionally. I encourage leaders to write their Leadership Agenda, a short (hopefully one-page) statement of their style of leadership. Writing a Leadership Agenda makes you an intentional leader.

Does being intentional make you authentic to your intentions?

Unfortunately, no! Anybody can write the most glorious intentions on a piece of paper. The difficult part is to live it in your day-to-day life. You have to become what you intend to be. That is what makes you authentic. Intentionality is exactly what it says: intent not reality. It's only when you realize your intentions that you become authentic. Intentionality is a necessary, but not a sufficient, condition for authenticity.

I'm often asked whether a Leadership Agenda should be about who you are or who you would like to be.

If intentionality is a precursor to authenticity, should your intentionality reflect who you are today so that you can be authentic to it?

I advise leaders to create in their Leadership Agenda a delicate balance of reality and aspirations – enough reality for it to be credible to others and enough aspiration for it to be inspirational to themselves. In my own Leadership Agenda, I proclaim, "Elevate the truth, without blame or judgment." Most who know me would attest to my authenticity in living the first half of that claim. I wish I could get a similar level of endorsement for the second half.

I also advise leaders to not only write down their leadership intentions but also vocalize them.

Vocalizing your intentions could take many forms and might address varied audiences. It could be a full-blown presentation to a group of employees, or it could be a phrase you intentionally refer to in hallway conversations. It could be an elevator pitch of your intentions that you repeatedly invoke, or it could be a behavior, called for by your intentions, that you repeatedly demonstrate.

For example, I repeatedly say that my style of leadership is to "Question the obvious, rationalize the outrageous and ponder the consequences."

David Baker, CEO of Think Shift, says, "Be the first to clap," in his Leadership Agenda. And he DOES! Every time!

Rob Connelly, president of Henny Penny says in his Leadership Agenda, "Savor the moment while always learning for a better tomorrow." By repeatedly invoking the phrase, he reminds others and himself of his intentions. Constant and repeated delivery (invocations) of your style of leadership serves two purposes. It tells everyone around you that you lead intentionally, and it also serves as a constant reminder to become what you intend to be.

Writing a Leadership Agenda makes you intentional. Delivering your Leadership Agenda makes you authentic.

For those of you who have written a Leadership Agenda, this should serve as a reminder to constantly deliver it. For those of you who have not written one, consider writing your Leadership Agenda. Intentionality is a precursor to authenticity, but authenticity should be your goal. Authenticity is a way of being – a way of being authentic to your intentions.

Authenticity Index

September 2014

Recently, the tragic death of Robin Williams created a lot of conversation online. While much of the conversation was probably respectful and filled with fond memories of the talented comedian, there were a number of posts in social media that were outright rude. So much so that his daughter, Zelda Williams, chose to close her Twitter account. She simply couldn't take it anymore.

Why do people feel comfortable saying things online they would probably never say to someone's face?

Do we all revert to a more primitive state when behind the shield of anonymity? This article is motivated by *Dealing with Digital Cruelty,* a recent Sunday Review article by Stephanie Rosenbloom in *The New York Times.*

Last winter, I was in Chicago during one of their many intensely frigid days. While riding the train, I discussed one of my crazy ideas with a Chicago native.

What if the CTA network were purely based on an honor system, I wondered.

People are expected to buy a ticket, but the Chicago Transit Authorities will never ask you to produce a ticket. "What percentage of the ridership would actually buy a ticket?" I asked my friend.

My cynical friend had this immediate response. "In Chicago? Maybe 10 percent will buy a ticket. All you tourists will buy one."

I then wondered how that behavior would change if there were some visible evidence of having bought a ticket. Say, your face glows red for the next two hours, so everybody on the train who had bought a ticket would be glowing red. "What percentage of the ridership would buy a ticket then?" I asked my friend.

His response: "Upwards of 90 percent."

What changed between the two hypothetical scenarios? **Transparency!** Transparency is the best form of accountability.

Let's try another thought experiment.

Imagine two strangers, both decent people, walking up simultaneously to the front doors of a tall skyscraper on a cold windy day in downtown Chicago. You would expect one to hold the door open for the other. But imagine their behavior later that evening in rush hour traffic. Both are behind the wheels of their cars, comfortably seated with their tinted windows and heated seats, driving in two different lanes and merging into one. How do they behave? Each would be trying to edge ahead of the other. Why the difference in their behavior? Transparency versus anonymity.

Anonymity can even occur in face-to-face interactions if you're anonymous to the people around you.

My wife recalls a story, many holidays ago, when our children were visiting us in Portland. Peppermint-candy ice cream is a popular holiday tradition for my family and often in short supply at the grocery store. Struggling to find a carton in the freezer aisle, my wife commented to another female shopper who just arrived how difficult it was to find peppermint-candy ice cream. The other lady spotted a stray carton in the adjacent shelf. Right in front of my wife, she grabbed it and walked away. Part frustrated and part infuriated, my wife abandoned her search. As she was standing at the cashier line, a man walked up to her, handed her a carton of the ice cream and asked, "Ma'am, is this what you were looking for?"

If that lady knew my wife, would she have acted the same way? What about that Good Samaritan?

He was an anonymous bystander who would have acted just as kindly had he been standing in that lady's place. While I was writing and editing this article, an interesting thing happened to me that prompted me to add this last thought. As I was settling into my aisle seat on an airplane, I noticed a mother in the middle seat two rows back trying to calm her little child who was sitting in the middle seat next to me. Clearly, the two had been separated. I offered to trade seats with the mother. As I squeezed into her cramped middle seat I wondered, would I have done that if the whole transaction were anonymous? I don't know.

Do we all behave differently when our behavior is transparent, not anonymous?

How often does that occur? Are some people more likely to behave authentically, whether or not it's transparent?

This inspired me to create an **Authenticity Index**: the percentage of instances of anonymous behaviors that would have been the same had the situation been transparent. I believe that some people have a high authenticity index while others don't fare as well. Some people are just fundamentally nice, some are nice because it is the right thing to do and yet others are nice because it is what society expects us to do. Each of those people's authenticity index is different.

But don't confuse authenticity with integrity.

A drug dealer who cheats and lies might have a high authenticity index, because he cheats and lies whether somebody is looking or not. I would like to think that most of our readers would not cheat or steal, whether or not somebody is looking. Yet my cynicism shows in the rush hour traffic example.

In keeping with the provocative nature of these articles, let me confess something many would disagree with.

I personally do not care for anonymous feedback. For example, in seeking written feedback at the end of my workshops, I insist that people identify themselves. I acknowledge that some people might be inhibited from saying what they really think, but should I care to receive the opinion of people with a low authenticity index?

Ask yourself, "What is my authenticity index?"

Even if you cannot associate an absolute number, you can probably compare two individuals and examine who might have a higher authenticity index. Under what anonymous circumstances do you behave differently? Why? Just that self-reflection can cause you to become intentional. I'm not suggesting that you change your behavior, just that you become intentional about your behavior. Intentionality causes you to become the leader you want to be.

Stewardship is a Precursor to Leadership

September 2011

I preface this article with a warning. This article uses Warren Buffet's personal position as an example of stewardship. The intent of this article is not to pass judgment on his position, specifically on taxation, but rather to use it as an illustration.

This month's *Food for Thought* is inspired by Warren Buffett's article *Stop Coddling the Super-Rich*, which appeared in *The New York Times* a couple of weeks ago. Buffett argues that rich people in the U.S. have a stewardship responsibility to carry a larger share of the federal tax burden, and legislators in Washington, D.C., have a stewardship responsibility to require it. Independent of your views on whether or not U.S. federal taxes are already too high, Buffett's argument is that the tax loopholes awarded to the rich have caused people with lower incomes to pay a disproportionate share of the taxes the government collects. So at a minimum, he would argue, even the current amount of taxes being collected should be redistributed.

I'm not here to stir up a political debate on taxation in the United States. (Almost half of my readers live outside the U.S. and likely couldn't care less.)

I'd rather argue that demonstration of stewardship is a fundamental requirement for people to acknowledge and respect leadership.

This applies to all leaders, whether they're political, business, civic, religious or otherwise. Not surprisingly, I will focus this conversation on business leaders – both corporations and individuals.

"Hold on," you might reply. "Isn't your claim, 'stewardship is a precursor to leadership,' just another example of motherhood and apple pie?" (See page 63 for definitions.) "Aren't these *Food for Thought* articles supposed to be controversial and provocative?"

Yes, indeed. Few would argue with the title of this article. But I intend to raise some poignant questions, forcing you to question whether you're discharging your stewardship responsibilities.

Has General Electric demonstrated its stewardship responsibility to the communities it serves? Over the last three years it has reported a total worldwide tax provision of $1 billion on a total three-year income of $44 billion, a meager two percent annual rate. Should one argue that GE has fully discharged its stewardship responsibility to its shareholders by creating a very tax efficient financial structure, thereby maximizing its return to the shareholders? Buffett asked if he discharged his stewardship responsibility last year when he was only required to pay 17 percent of his earnings in taxes, while each of the other 20 people in his office paid somewhere between 33 percent and 41 percent of their income.

Has the leadership of a corporation, one that paid lower bonuses to all employees during a less than stellar year, discharged its stewardship responsibilities when the leadership had more to do with the poor performance than lower level employees?

While both Walmart and Dell put a lot of pressure on their vendors to reduce prices, Dell insists on knowing how the vendor is going to accomplish that by taking costs out of the supply chain. Is Walmart discharging stewardship responsibility to its vendors or is it just squeezing and recycling its vendors? Are companies like Starbucks (that have a generous health insurance policy), Pret A Manger (that empowers its in-store employees with cash and non-cash incentives) and Chick-fil-A (which demonstrates its Christian values throughout its operations) demonstrating stewardship? If so, is it at a cost to the shareholders and/or employees? In case you think I only throw stones at others, let me shatter this glass house as well. In a society like the U.S., where the structure of the healthcare system is for the employers to provide health insurance, has a small company (like LogiStyle) that does not offer health insurance to its employees (in LogiStyle's case, three), discharged their stewardship responsibilities?

Is stewardship a cost you incur to be a good citizen? I would argue otherwise.

Starbucks and Pret A Manger come out ahead with their more expensive employee policies. Just compare the workforce morale and the employee turnover of those companies versus your average fast food establishments. You don't have to know the numbers – as a customer, you can see it in the spirit of the employees! Dell comes out ahead by insisting on knowing how the vendors take cost out of the system. Buffett's argument is that when stewardship is not in the leader's self-interest (such as for GE and Buffett, who are both required to maximize their benefits by taking all legal and ethical means) the society (i.e. the government) has an obligation to structure the laws to impose such stewardship.

Stewardship gives leadership higher leverage to accomplish their purpose. And when good stewardship is not in your self-interest, leaders have the stewardship responsibility to ask the society to impose them, as demonstrated by Warren Buffett.

I wrote this article to urge you, a leader, to ask questions about stewardship that are relevant to your situation.

I suggest you discuss the issue with the constituents for whom you are a steward. If you're hesitant to discuss these issues with them, then ask yourself, "What do I fear?" Open conversations like this only heighten the sensitivities of the constituents and the responsibility of the stewards. At my company, I intend to do just that.

Boards

Corporate boards are governance bodies. Unlike executive teams, they are not executive bodies. I have served on a number of boards, public and private, for-profit and non-profit.

The directors usually have extensive executive experience, often in related disciplines, markets and businesses of the companies they govern. There is a natural tendency to suggest how the business might be run. After all, they have been there and done that. The executive team members roll their eyes.

How should directors contribute without becoming executives? There is no easy answer. As I went through my experience in the boards I served, questions arose in my mind and they spawned some of the ideas in this chapter.

Should the Board Get Involved in Strategic Planning?

September 2008

This topic should be particularly relevant to directors on boards of small- to mid-cap public companies. These organizations typically operate in well-defined markets and likely aren't large conglomerates. In these companies, many directors are either former CEOs or have served in a senior operating capacity, often in related markets and businesses. And, much to management's chagrin, these directors are tempted to make meaningful contributions to the company's strategic plan. Management silently laments that these directors lack the necessary understanding of the current markets and the current business, the intimacy with organizational capabilities or the responsibility required for developing a viable strategic plan. Directors should let management develop and present the best organic strategic plan they can, a plan based on the assumption that the company will continue as a going concern with the current management team in charge. Let's call this Option A.

What, then, is the role of the board in the strategic planning process? It's actually quite significant – not in the creation of the plan, but in evaluating it. The board should ask management to provide not only an organic plan (Option A) but a set of strategic alternatives (Option B). Violating the previous assumption that the company remains a going concern in its current form, the strategic alternatives should include a spectrum of possibilities, ranging from breaking up the company by selling detachable pieces, to selling the whole company.

The board's job is to evaluate Option A, considering its potential optimism and long-term execution risk, and compare it against Option B, considering the immediate payoff it might offer to shareholders. But wait! We're not done yet. The board should *then* compare these two options against a third option, Option C. Option C is a hypothetical analysis, conducted by the independent directors of the board, examining what a new management team might propose if they were brought into the company. The board's role in strategic planning is to evaluate these three options and choose a direction for the company.

Too often, directors become so attached to the company that it becomes their identity. These directors ignore their role in evaluating Options B and C, and instead get intimately involved in Option A, the organic strategic plan. Rarely do boards proactively examine Option C until it becomes a reality. When the board examines all three options during each annual strategic planning cycle, it allows the board to contribute in a broader way. The board can govern the company's management rather than meddle with management's responsibility – developing an organic strategic plan.

Can Your Board Face Warren Buffett?

May 2008

We each have a favorite example of a poorly performing public company with an entrenched board. We wonder why, after so many quarters of poor performance, they still haven't taken any action. This behavior seems to be more common among smaller public companies that fly below the radar of corporate raiders and big private equity firms. Here's a provocative exercise for boards of smaller public companies that don't want to fall into a similar pattern.

While directors of small public company boards are accountable to shareholders, they are in no practical danger of being thrown out of the job. Directors like these should ask themselves if they would survive a form of rigorous scrutiny that I call the Warren Buffett test.

Warren Buffett is merely used as an icon of smart, simple investing with a no-nonsense, no-hype attitude. Imagine that your company is entirely owned by Warren Buffett, who has left the board and management intact. Furthermore, imagine that the chairman of the board (or the lead independent director) had to fly to Omaha, Nebraska, and meet with Buffett after every board meeting to explain the performance of the company and what the board and management are doing to improve it. Ask yourself questions you think Buffett would ask and discuss whether he would be as patient with the board as you are with management. This discussion could even be conducted during the independent directors' session with one of the directors assuming Buffett's role. If this exercise is done with integrity, it will make directors of poorly performing companies rethink their approach.

Three's a Crowd: When CEOs Need to Bow Out of a Conversation

June 2007

Long before director institutes started popping up – even before Sarbanes-Oxley – Cynthia Richson and her colleagues at the State of Wisconsin Investment Board (SWIB) organized one of the first ever director conferences in support of shareholders. At one of its early incarnations, Bill George, former chairman and CEO of Medtronic, spoke about good governance practices. I credit him for planting the seed that grew into this piece.

As a good governance practice, I encourage routine one-on-one conversations between each director on the board of a public company and each senior executive reporting to the CEO.

In any public company, the CEO, CFO and general counsel usually have direct access to the board. Surprisingly, in some companies, the board's access to management ends there! These companies aside, CEOs of most companies provide "controlled access" to the operating executives. Controlled access might include opportunities for management to make presentations to the directors at board meetings. Mind you, these presentations have undoubtedly been scrutinized by and rehearsed for the CEO. Controlled access might include participation in social events – where the CEO is at the other end of the room. Or it might even include an occasional email between an operating executive and a director with a copy sent to the CEO. In all of these kinds of interactions, the executive – even well intentioned executives in good companies – are likely to be mindful of what the CEO would want them to say. Just that simple psychological constraint seriously taints the nature of the interaction.

I am often asked by boards of directors to come and share progressive ideas for good governance.

One of the practices I advocate is establishing routine one-on-one conversations between operating executives and directors. These conversations, conducted without an agenda or resulting actions, give insight into operating executives' thought processes. The personal frustrations of the sales VP, the division president's informal report on the challenges in gaining market share, or what keeps the manufacturing VP awake at night are all insights that are unlikely to surface in orchestrated management presentations to the board. Yet collectively – through the many one-on-one conversations between directors and management – the board can get a better sense of management's thinking and the challenges they face.

For this process to be effective, clear protocols need to be established on all sides – the CEO, the directors and the executives.

The CEO should set up the practice and then get out of the way. The directors need to be educated on listening and asking questions without providing any directive. Even opinions, when expressed strongly, can be construed as directives by the executive. The director has an obligation to emphasize otherwise. Management, in turn, needs to be totally candid and share any details requested by the director. In public companies where this practice has been systematically followed, the board is better connected with management. Still, it takes a confident CEO to institute the practice.

Lastly, this practice of "skip level" one-on-one conversations is just as useful and effective within the management hierarchy of the company and is more often practiced at that level. At a recent meeting of corporate directors, someone observed that even the CEOs who encourage this practice within their company's management hierarchy seem to be more reticent in promoting it at the board level. But these CEOs should ask themselves, how many times has someone in my company said – to me or someone else – what they thought I wanted to hear? And, out of those instances, how many times did they not say something I needed to hear?

Dissatisfied Shareholders – What Recourse Do They Have?

July 2009

What recourse do activist shareholders of public companies have when they are dissatisfied with their board?

Can they take them to court?

Citing the **business judgment rule**, the courts have been reluctant to second-guess a board's decisions as long as board members have discharged their duty of loyalty and duty of care. The courts have maintained that the shareholders' only recourse is to elect a different board. The shareholders have complained that, with the company's proxy controlled by the incumbent board, it's difficult, if not impossible, to oust or replace sitting directors. In turn, shareholders have sought access to the company's proxy. The recent upheaval in corporate America and the resulting pressure for reform on Congress has resulted in a recent proposal by the U.S. Securities and Exchange Commission (SEC) to provide proxy access to "significant" shareholders. Directors rebut that providing proxy access to shareholders will result in nominations representing singular agendas that are not in the interest of the larger shareholder base.

With that as the backdrop, I offer you a provocative and controversial idea.

What if the SEC required public companies' corporate boards to nominate more candidates than they needed, say in excess of at least 25 percent, failing which the boards must accede proxy access to "significant" shareholders, as currently proposed by the SEC?

This proposal would ensure that the shareholders have a real choice in the proxy, and yet still allow the board to ensure that nominated candidates represent the broader interests of shareholders. The slated candidates will invariably provide an alternative to current directors. Activist shareholders can then remove sitting directors they're dissatisfied with, causing every director to be more vigilant about shareholders' interests. Of course, the company and the proxy statement would have to be restricted from using its resources and reach to advocate or advance the candidacy of any specific director.

Directors are likely to complain that such a beauty-contest-proxy will dissuade qualified candidates from serving as directors. They might also argue that the collegial atmosphere of the boardroom might be compromised with each director only interested in their re-election. In my opinion, some turmoil and change in the boardroom and some level of instability in a director's tenure and re-election might not be such a bad thing.

Strategy

This chapter has a lot of articles that were timely for the events of the moment. The stock market crashed in 2008 as a result of sub-prime mortgages and the collapse of the banking industry. Companies hunkered down and regrouped. Everybody had to clean up their houses and become more efficient – the silver lining of a recession. During that time companies became risk averse. So a lot of the articles are about the advantage of being "one step ahead." In that namesake article, I was tempted to reflect my interest in magic by applying it to business.

How is it that some companies execute a strategy whereby they repeatedly introduce new and compelling products, and some companies are a one-hit wonder? How is it that some companies fall and recover while others rest on their laurels? In this chapter, the article on how Apple would run your business should make you think about that.

Finally, I want to talk about left-brain creativity. Of course, there is no left or right brain distinction, other than in the folklore that it has created. It has always bothered me that we associate creativity with the arts. Like in any advertising business, we have a creative group at our company. They do all the graphic design, the creative drawings, the videos and presentations and everything else that you would associate with the creative group. And they do wonderful work. As I give my talks around the continent, I often show some of the material we have created for other companies. Clients are always impressed. It gives me pride to show their work. But I have always wondered if they are as creative as the scientists that I used to work with in my high-tech days. Is there a difference in the creativity of the artist and the scientist? What is creativity anyway? We talk about it in this chapter.

2011: A Year to Focus on the Balance Sheet

January 2011

The late Sir James Goldsmith, an outspoken corporate raider in his time, used to jokingly call himself the "Ajax" of corporate America. Claiming that he knew of no well-run company that had been subjected to a corporate raid, he would say that corporations under attack end up adopting the very ideas advanced by corporate raiders – even in cases where the raider doesn't succeed. His point was that stagnant corporations become inefficient and complacent unless external forces cause them to change and he was that external "Ajax" of corporate America, forcing corporations to adapt.

A depressed economy, like the one we've experienced over the past couple of years, might be a less threatening but equally painful Ajax.

Most corporations that survived the economy did so by becoming more lean and efficient. And they are, in some sense, the better for it. If, as most economists predict, the economy should turn for the better in 2011, your income statements should take a positive turn. And a healthy and growing business can forgive a lot of sins. But watch out! Don't let the balance sheet slide.

I am not referring to the financial balance sheet, but rather the non-financial intangible assets that you have created. More on this topic is discussed in *Do You Focus on the Income Statement or the Balance Sheet?* (See page 29). A lean operation running efficiently is an intangible asset not represented in your financial balance sheet. Furthermore, if your business is healthy and growing, make sure you focus on building new intangible assets that will serve you for a long time. Consider a more efficient supply chain or more streamlined business processes. Invest in your people. A growing business is the best time and place to grow people. Give them "stretch" opportunities.

What non-financial balance sheet goals do you have for 2011?

My friend and colleague, Dave Coreson, who has run global, billion-dollar manufacturing operations, experimented with a simple exercise: He wanted new people in old jobs. So when he took over a new manufacturing operation, he asked everyone at his staff meeting to stand up, move over one seat and sit down. He told them they had a new job – the job of the person whose seat they were in. Clearly, he had to make some minor adjustments. But he sent a clear message: both people and positions have to grow. Dave always left behind a richer set of intangible, balance sheet assets than what he inherited in any role he stepped into.

So ask yourself how you will enrich your balance sheet in 2011. While focusing on the income statement might be easier in 2011, it's what you do with your balance sheet that will speak volumes in the years ahead.

Do You Expect a Recovery in 2012?

January 2012

Let me break the mood by asking you a question: Will there be a recovery in 2012?

I'm not going to prophesize, but I will draw on some of my previous *Food for Thought* ideas and offer three provocative actions for those of you who believe 2012 will bring a recovery.

Act before the next guy does:

Act on your belief before others do – before it becomes a commonly held belief. You need to be one step ahead of your competition, as I mentioned in *One Step Ahead* on page 56. Don't wait until everybody else starts acting or you'll lose your advantage. (I often advise business leaders to stop wasting time reading business books that others recommend. If somebody recommends it, the information inside is probably popular knowledge by now. Be the first to read one and recommend it to others instead.) So make that hire to grow your business. Start that project that you think will generate additional revenue. Buy that company before your 2012 belief becomes a reality.

Take risks:

If you believe a recovery is coming in 2012, now is the time to take risks. In these economic times, most people and businesses have become more risk-intolerant. If you have the means to take risks, you can actually garner greater rewards for a given level of risk than you could have in steadier economic times. That's why you should demand a greater reward but be more willing to take risks. See *In This Economy, Don't Become Risk Averse* on page 58.

Don't get bloated:

Corporate profits in the U.S. are at record levels, while unemployment continues to run high. Why is that? The late Sir James Goldsmith used to say, "Raiders and recessions cleanse companies." After the recession, in 2009, bloated corporate organizations were forced to become more efficient. As the economy improved, their revenues grew, but they maintained their efficiency.

They did more with less and with fewer people. The lesson: If you decide to invest, make sure you don't get bloated. Every time you make an investment, look for half the investment dollars from efficiencies in other parts of the organization. To grow muscle, you have to cut the fat.

One Step Ahead

February 2012

Joann Lublin, a reporter for *The Wall Street Journal*, responded to *Do You Expect a Recovery in 2012?* (See page 54) and pointed to an interview she did with Ram Charan, the renowned management consultant. Ram Charan's comments in the article titled *Message to CEOs: Do More to Keep Your Key Employees* have inspired me to write this piece.

I'll start by revealing the secrets of a genre of magic tricks that I like to call "One Step Ahead."

One such trick in this genre involves a pack of cards. The idea is to spread the cards face down on a table until they appear to be randomly distributed. The magician then points to a random card, declares its value and draws the card into his hand. The magician does this three times over, pointing to three different cards. Then, to prove his magical powers, he reveals the three cards to his audience. Voila! They are precisely the cards the magician had predicted!

The trick:

Before spreading the cards on the table, the magician notes one card in the deck. For this example, I'll say it's the 2♠. The magician tracks movement of the 2♠ as he spreads the deck on the table. Pointing to a random card in the deck, the magician declares it to be 2♠ picks it up and looks at it. Noting its value, let's say 7♦, he points to another random card and declares it to be 7♦. The magician picks this second card up. Noting its value, say Q♥, the magician points to the card he knows to be 2♠, declares it to be Q♥ and places this last card in his hand. Lo and behold the three cards he holds in his hands are precisely the three values he announced. The magician was just one step ahead of the audience the whole time.

What does this have to do with management, business and leadership?

Are you always one step ahead of your market? In some sense, this is the point Ram Charan is making in his interview with Joann Lublin. He argues that this is the time to be aggressive with key talent in the marketplace – both in retaining your talent and hiring new talent. Business leaders need to recognize that, even though the economic conditions have been fragile over the past few years, they need to compensate their key employees based on what the next year will bring, not just what last year looked like. You need to be aggressive in hiring and retaining good talent six months before the market becomes aggressive.

For example, a year ago in the energy industry around Calgary, Alberta, you would have been able to pick up high-quality engineering talent quite easily. Yet try getting good engineering talent now! Everybody is scrambling for more engineers.

To protect yourself from downturns in the economy, like the magic trick, you need to identify a 2♠ that you can keep on stand-by.

If you identify a business need that isn't urgent, but is worthy of pursuit – a cost reduction or process improvement project, a desired feature enhancements in your products, etc. – then you can do exactly what the magician does. You can be aggressive in the market, constantly taking a step in anticipation, and when the market slows down, you can use your resources for the stand-by project. Of course, resources are not always interchangeable, but this concept of "One Step Ahead" makes you think differently.

In This Economy, Don't Become Risk Averse

May 2009

In this economy, it might seem reasonable to be less tolerant of risk, but be wary of becoming risk averse. In fact, I claim that if you have the capacity to take risks, this is the best time to be embracing it – the rewards are actually higher when others are risk-intolerant!

But first, let's be clear with what constitutes risk and reward.

Risk is the uncertainty of future outcomes. To put it more technically, risk is the standard deviation of the economic values of possible future outcomes. Reward is the expected value (mean) of those possible outcomes. Each of us and each of our organizations have a risk-reward profile (i.e. a graph that shows the minimum amount of reward we look for in taking on a level of risk). People and organizations are more risk-tolerant when they accept a lower level of reward for a certain level of risk.

In these economic times, most people and businesses have become less tolerant of risk.

If you have the means to take risk, you can actually garner a greater reward for a given level of risk than you could have in steadier economic times. That's why you should demand a greater reward while being more open to taking risks.

Let's illustrate this with a few concrete business examples. If you are a roofing contractor and you come across a job that you otherwise might have shunned because of the complications and "gotchas" involved, now you might seriously consider the job because you can command a higher price for it. Remember, like you, most people are weary and there are fewer bidders for that job. Likewise, if you are considering a risky acquisition, don't walk away just because it's risky. Demand a higher reward for taking that risk because it might be available in this economy. This is the logic that has led private investors to gobble up many of the toxic default swap loans in bank auctions. The discount on those loans – a proxy for the reward – has made them very attractive.

Needless to say, if you don't have the capacity to take risk, this discussion is moot, but if you do, this is the best time to seek out opportunities. The rewards are plenty.

Now Is the Time to Invest in Your Business

March 2009

The current economic crisis has caused all of us to stop and reflect. Most businesses are negatively impacted and it's only reasonable to carefully manage all discretionary costs. Eventually the economy will rebound, but for now you're probably resigned to hunker down and wait it out.

Yet I am advising clients to invest – prudently and strategically.

Make those investments that you might have otherwise deferred so that you're poised to change the landscape when the economy recovers. It's in times like these that most markets' competitive landscapes change. And that's your opportunity to emerge as a more strategic and powerful player. I'm not suggesting that you spend freely. On the contrary, I recommend controlling discretionary expenses even tighter. Be even more frugal and use the savings to invest more strategically.

Do you know what strategic investments you could make right now that would position you as a more competitive player when the economy rebounds?

I guarantee that having that discussion with your executive team will be valuable. Do you have the financial capacity to make those investments? This is the time to examine what non-strategic expenses can be curtailed to make room for those strategic ones. Do you have the courage to make those strategic investments? That is what separates leaders from followers.

I've taken my own medicine and have analyzed what strategic investments I should make and how to fund them. This has given me a whole new perspective on the economic downturn.

Let's All Sequester

March 2013

My friend Glenn Mangurian and I think alike. Yet we also think very differently. Glenn writes a column called *Pushing the Edge* and titled this month's piece *Sequester This*, with some interesting ideas on how to force U.S. politicians to compromise and solve the sequester. I, on the other hand, am going to write about why you should promote the **sequester** idea in your business.

First, I should apologize to my foreign readers who may not even understand this specific use of the word "sequester."

After all, most of us in the U.S. had not heard of it either until a couple of months ago. I also apologize for repeatedly using United States politics as a source for business ideas. The current U.S. political landscape offers so much fodder for creative, controversial and provocative ideas that it's hard to resist.

Here's a backgrounder for my foreign friends: To avoid the automatic expiration of some attractive tax cuts at the end of 2012 (then called the Fiscal Cliff) Congress agreed to extend a portion of those tax cuts, on the condition that Congress could come to an agreement on a deficit reduction package by March 1. To force that to happen, Congress imposed automatic, across-the-board budget cuts (with some exceptions) on the assumption that they were so onerous that the elected officials would be forced to find a better compromise. These across-the-board budget cuts have come to be called the sequester.

I want to advocate the use of the sequester in your annual operating budgets.

But first, let's remind ourselves of the concept of **zero-base budgeting**. This was popular a few decades ago and many companies claimed to use it. However, I contend that few, if any, ever did. The concept of zero-base budgeting is to assume that none of the previous year's expenses of each department are automatically carried over into the next year. You start from zero and justify every piece of expense in your budget. While the concept has a lot of merit, it requires a lot of work. In effect, you would have to take everything out of your house and put it on the lawn, then use a fixed amount of Monopoly money to buy each desired item and bring it back into the house. That includes furniture, people, vendors and every other possible expense. While it is ideologically sound, it is practically infeasible. So most companies that claimed to practice it assumed that most of the stuff in the lawn would come back into the house.

Here's a different idea I've practiced in a few companies.

We now call it **sequestration**, though we did not know the term when we practiced it. At the annual budgeting time, give every department an automatic 10 percent budget cut. Tell them that there is probably enough fat in each department for the executives to cut 10 percent. To keep your executives from yelling "Fire!" tell them that you will be judging them based on the wisdom of their cuts. Then, with the stick in one hand, extend a juicy carrot with the other. Tell them that you now have X million dollars for a strategic investment, and ask your executives for proposals on where you might invest it.

Sequestration is more practical than zero-base budgeting. Each manager can do this within their departments, and they can do so with insight into the cost and value of the expenses they're incurring. You can make repeated strategic investments while minimizing the amount of frugality needed to do it. It enables you to create a lean organization.

Couple Strategic Investments with Spending Cuts

September 2010

One silver lining of the economic recession is that surviving businesses usually become lean and efficient – recession is like the Ajax of business! However, when the economy improves and you decide to make some focused strategic investments in your business, you run the risk of your managers letting their guard down on being frugal. **My advice: couple strategic investments in focused areas with across the board spending cuts.** Let me explain.

One of the best ways to clean your house of junk is to move all of your possessions out into the yard and bring back exactly those items you wish to keep. In budgeting, this is called zero-base budgeting, where every department starts out the year with a zero budget and has to justify every bit of planned expense. Although zero-base budgeting is powerful and effective (imagine if our government did that!), it is painful, arduous and time-consuming. As a result, most managers try to adopt the concept of zero-base budgeting without actually doing it. The result: a far cry from its true value. The problem is that zero-base budgeting, in its true sense, is not practical. So we offer a pragmatic approach that uses a similar principle.

Let's say, coming out of this recession, you decide to make a two million dollar investment in a strategic area. Get your executive team to agree that this strategic investment is the right thing to do for the business. Having received their support, ask them to find half a million dollars of savings elsewhere in the company and offer to match three for one – as investment in that strategic area – every dollar of savings they create in the rest of the company. Notice your outlay of expenses remain the same as you originally had intended. But this approach keeps the pressure on the rest of the organization to be frugal, gives them a role in funding this strategic investment, and makes sure that the beneficiary of the investment spends every dollar wisely as the rest of the company watches like a hawk. In other words, couple strategic investments with spending cuts – it is to the benefit of all.

Take All That Motherhood and Apple Pie Out of Your Strategic Plan

April 2007

Strategic plans are often full of motherhood and apple pie: non-controversial comments and observations that are widely known and generally accepted. You're probably more familiar with them than you realize. Examples include, "Markets are getting increasingly competitive," and "Design cycles and time-to-market are shortening." In an attempt to make the strategic plan comprehensive, an inordinate amount of time is spent documenting what is already known. Worst of all, precious little effort is spent on those few critical but potentially controversial decisions that are key to the strategic future of the company.

Strategic plans must stare controversy in the face and choose to either accept the status quo or make a controversial decision.

Without controversy, decisions are seldom strategic. For example, if it's obvious that the business needs an additional manufacturing plant and the strategic plan calls for building one, it's not a strategic decision. It's a tactical one. A decision to build an additional plant is strategic only if some people in the management team think it's unnecessary, thus creating controversy.

I promote a methodology for strategic planning called FIR: Forks-In-the-Road.

Management selects a few critical forks in the road where there is internal controversy on which path to take. The selection of the forks and the choice made at each fork become the focus of the strategic planning process, the results of which become the crux of the strategic plan. Stanford professor Robert Burgelman calls these choices "irreversible commitments," essential ingredients for effective strategic planning.

In companies where I've implemented this methodology, management spends more time focusing on the significant issues facing the business. Their strategies, now free of motherhood and apple pie, are less meaningful to outsiders (such as a potential strategic buyer of the company) but are more useful to the internal management team. But if you still like your strategic plans topped off with a generous layer of whipped cream, fluffed up with a lot of air, I suggest including a five-year financial projection resulting from the FIR choices you've made.

How Would Apple Run Your Business?

May 2012

Glenn Mangurian writes a monthly piece called *Pushing the Edge,* similar to my *Food for Thought* articles. This article is inspired by his provocative issue from last month, titled *What if Apple bought General Motors?* Needless to say, credit for this entire piece goes to Glenn.

Apple has created a distinguished brand, reflected not only in its products but in its stores as well. And their brand has created an exceptionally loyal following among its customers. In May of 2012, Apple announced that they had almost doubled their earnings last quarter. Instead of asking why Apple is so greedy for profits or why they don't sell their products cheaper, those people who line up to protest the corporate greed of ExxonMobil, Walmart or Goldman Sachs instead line up around the block to buy the next iPhone or iPad! Walmart is taken to task for its labor practices. Even a venerable brand like Nike is pressured to address the working conditions in its offshore manufacturing plants. But Apple, faced with similar questions, goes almost scot-free! Why is that?

Apple's brand has been established through careful control of everything they do – not just the products they release. And I do mean everything they do – how they choose and interact with their vendors, how and when they communicate with their customers, and what they expect of their employees. In other words, they meticulously manage their culture. As a result, if you were to imagine Apple getting into the automobile business – which they might – you would probably have a pretty good idea of what an iCar might look like.

Let's take that thought to the next level – to consumer product companies beyond electronics. If Apple were to run Procter & Gamble or Campbell Soup, how would those companies change? Don't just think of how the products would change, but how the company itself would change. What if you went beyond consumer product companies? How about an elevator company? How would Apple run an Otis or KONE? What if Apple bought one of the many struggling airlines? How would the service and product of iAir be significantly different?

And so I ask, how would Apple run your company? It doesn't matter if you offer goods or services to consumers or businesses. Whatever you do, Apple would probably do it a bit differently – not necessarily better, but differently. You can probably already see how this thought experiment opens up your imagination. It's interesting and provocative because Apple has a very clear brand and culture, and we're all very familiar with it. But you could ask this question using any company's brand you're passionate about and clearly understand.

So ask that of your own company. After all, you have the passion and clearly understand your own brand. What if you bought one of your competitors or vertically integrated with somebody in your food chain? How would you run that company differently from how it's being run today? How would your brand cause that company to act and behave differently? Conversely, what if one of your competitors or a partner in your food chain bought your company? How would they run it differently?

Take any one of the questions asked above and ask each member of your executive team to prepare a vivid description of how your company would change. Then have a discussion with your team so that everyone can benefit from the multitude of perspectives. This is what Glenn Mangurian calls, *Pushing the Edge.*

Left-Brain Creativity Has More Economic Value

June 2015

In the article entitled *Mind those Q's* (See page 103), I intentionally omitted creativity in my list of Q's (types of intelligence), and left that discussion for another article. Since then, I've been thinking a lot about creativity, and I've gained enough conviction to make a provocative statement: left-brain creativity has more economic value than right-brain creativity.

What is left-brain creativity and how does it differ from right-brain creativity? What is creativity anyway?

Let's take some examples. Most people think of literature and the arts as creative activities. An artist is, of course, considered creative. A beautiful painting or sculpture, a touching poem or a striking arrangement of flowers is considered creative expression. Do you consider the street portrait painter, who whips up a remarkable resemblance of you in twenty minutes, creative? Or would you consider that person technically skilled with a formulaic process for the task, and call it "producing" rather than "creating" a portrait? Do you think a commercial graphic designer is engaged in creativity when, every day, they design brochures on demand?

Is that any more creative than the tax accountant who, with a quick study of your accounts, can tell you the legal tax breaks and deductions that can benefit you? Is the hedge fund manager – who, from a myriad of investment vehicles, develops an unusual derivative, providing a high return with low risk – not a creative individual? After all, nobody else had thought of that derivative and there was no existing formula for it. Is the scientist, who thinks of mixing a unique combination of chemicals to produce a polymer with attractive properties, not a creative individual? Are these accountants, bankers and scientists not creative? What is creativity, then?

Here's my definition: creativity is the process of extracting an *intriguing expression* from an *unstructured space* of infinite possibilities.

Let's illustrate this definition with traditional and non-traditional examples. Leonardo da Vinci extracted an intriguing expression, the Mona Lisa, out of a plain canvas. Margaret Mitchell's novel *Gone with the Wind* and David Selznick's screen adaptation are both intriguing expressions, one written on a blank piece of paper and the other imprinted on celluloid. Andy Warhol's questioning of, "What is art?" led him to the intriguing expression of his Campbell's soup can paintings. Famous advertising slogans such as "plop, plop, fizz, fizz," "don't leave home without it" and "reach out and touch someone" are all intriguing expressions, each with a significant impact and drawn from a blank slate.

Likewise, when Isaac Newton asked, "Did the apple fall to the earth or did the earth move to the apple?" he created an intriguing expression, the gravitational law, to conclude that both the apple and the earth moved toward each other. Magic Johnson, arguably the best point guard in NBA history, was a master in finding that sliver of a hole in the other team's defense, and that allowed him to make an intriguing expression, the bounce pass, resulting in baskets. Karl Marx, in abstracting the struggles of societies, created an intriguing expression, the struggle between the source of production and the means of production. Mahatma Gandhi's non-violent passive resistance was an intriguing expression (strategy) to fight the British. In all these cases, was there not an intriguing expression extracted from an unstructured space of infinite possibilities? That is creativity.

There's a common assumption that, when it comes to creative activities, you can tell a good outcome when you see it. But there's no real test for a good outcome.

In other words, the quality of the outcome is usually undefined, vague and often in the eyes of the beholder.

The crucial phrases in my definition of creativity are "intriguing expressions" and "unstructured space." My use of the word "intriguing" is a placeholder for this vague concept of goodness we attach to creative pursuits. In fact, in some situations (like the tax accountant, the hedge fund manager and the scientist) it can be more quantified than others (like the artist, poet, portrait painter and the graphic designer).

The second key phrase is "unstructured space." If the space of possibilities – even infinite possibilities – can be structured in an orderly fashion, and a mechanical search can be launched, assisted by computers, then the resulting solution is unlikely to be considered creative. When a painter starts with a blank piece of canvas, the painter's space of possibilities is infinite and totally unstructured. The same is true of a poet with a blank piece of paper. But the same is also true of the scientist trying to find a new polymer, or the hedge fund manager trying to find a new derivative. All of them acknowledge that the space of possibilities is infinite and unstructured, and they dream up a potentially intriguing solution out-of-the-blue, refining it with their technical skills to make it remarkable.

So it's the unstructured nature of the space of possibilities that makes the task creative. If the space of possibilities were structured, it would be mechanical.

To illustrate that, let's use a math example (Warning: math-phobic readers are advised to skip this paragraph). A perfect number is one whose proper divisors sum to the number in question. For example, the proper divisors of 6 are 1, 2 and 3, and the proper divisors of 28 are 1, 2, 4, 7 and 14. In both cases, the proper divisors sum to the number. The numbers 6 and 28 are the first two perfect numbers. The ancient Greeks identified and named them, and they knew of only four perfect numbers (496 and 8128). The Greeks believed the gods had made them perfect. Today, we know of 49 perfect numbers, the 49th of which has almost 35 million digits. Why are they important? Perfect numbers are related to Mersenne primes, which play a role in cryptography, including the RSA cryptosystem used to encrypt your credit card information over the internet. So finding the 50th perfect number would be of value. In fact, there is a globally distributed computing effort underway in search for the 50th perfect number. Would finding that number be a result of creativity or industry? Since the space of possible solutions (the numbers) is very structured, such a find would be viewed as the result of exhaustive work. Yet if somebody came up with a formula for perfect numbers, that would be creative!

If creativity is a search in an unstructured space, can we limit creativity by structuring the space? Yes, indeed!

For example, the street portrait painter might have an established process for measuring the size of your face and the relative positions of your eyes and nose to quickly zone in on a realistic image. The painter has used a process to limit the space of possibilities and brought structure to that space. The commercial graphic designer might be asked to bring structure to her process to get the task done on schedule. When the ad-man is searching for that right idea, he often brings structure to his thoughts by segmenting his audience, prioritizing them and looking at trends to guide his "creative." In other words, the ad-man brings structure to his space of possibilities, which limits his creativity.

Even though recent neuroscience has definitively debunked the idea of left-brain and right-brain thinking, I use these terms as a common placeholder. So I refer to math, science and analytical activities as left-brain, and art, music and subjective activities as right-brain.

Both types of activities can be creative. And the myth that left-brain activities are not creative might actually be harming us.

Do you ever ask your accountant to be creative – I don't mean illegal – but legally creative? If you do, she might find you opportunities for savings or economies of scale. Do you look for a creative way to segment your market, as opposed to the traditional segmentations along industry, products, applications, channels, customers, etc.? A creative segmentation might provide more insight than a traditional segmentation. Do you look for creativity in your investment strategy? These are examples of left-brain creativity.

Left-brain creativity often has a more objective definition for the term "intriguing expression." In other words, the results are more measurable.

When a creative accountant suggests that you combine the data processing of sales and service to increase the leads for service opportunities, the result of that creativity is more objective. When you come up with an investment strategy that correlates the currency of the investment with countries where you do business, the resulting hedge is clearly seen. The goodness of the results is objective and not just in the eyes of the beholder.

In contrast, right-brain creativity is often subjective. Conceptual artists Damien Hirst and Andres Serrano might be well-known artists for their controversial work, and the art community would certainly consider their art creative, but it's unlikely that most who see it will appreciate their work. And, certainly, young emerging artists working in that genre are unlikely to be a commercial success – or even eke out a living like the less creative street portrait painter.

In other words, the subjective goodness of right-brain creativity gives it less economic value than left-brain creativity. (Of course this is not a commentary on its social value.)

In business, we should encourage left-brain creativity in functions and activities that are otherwise not considered creative. Even technical tasks can lead to intriguing expressions.

Compensation

Compensation has been a hot topic in these articles. They have all revolved around one theme: Do you differentiate your pay to reflect performance? People tend to track the average pay of their employees or the average percent increase given to employees. Seldom does management look at the standard deviation of the pay or of the increases. Which would you like: a small standard deviation or a large standard deviation?

A quick reflection reveals that a large standard deviation will represent the high performers being appropriately rewarded in comparison to the low performers. Yet the only way to achieve a high standard deviation and maintain a prescribed average is to award some people a lot at the expense of others receiving little to nothing. Are we, as management, willing to do that?

In this chapter, we also talk about stock options. In my opinion, the high tech boom of the late last century erroneously viewed stock options as free money. Prior to the FASB 123(R) ruling, stock options did not show up as an expense on the income statement. So companies compensated their employees using a currency that hurt the shareholders but did not reflect badly on management. They thought they were printing money. The articles in this chapter talk about the cost of stock options.

Variable Compensation: Incentive, Bonus or a Reward?

January 2014

This topic is inspired, in part, by a discussion I had with my staff at our planning meeting a month ago as we were massaging our variable compensation program for this year. And, about a week later, my friend Gerhard Beenen sent me a *PBS NewsHour* article by Paul Solman called *Why Not Give Money Instead of a Gift?*, which added some fodder. Finally, given that many of you might be planning your compensation programs for this year, I thought this topic might be especially appropriate.

Is there value to supplementing base compensation with variable compensation?

Do you have a variable compensation program in your company? Although the employer benefits by indexing a portion of the employees' compensation to the performance of the company, does it inspire the intended behavior in employees? Is variable compensation an incentive, bonus or reward? To explore this, let's focus on the distinction between the three in the context of variable compensation for employees.

An incentive is a contractual agreement (written or verbal) in which the employer sets certain predetermined goals. Upon achieving those goals, the employee is entitled to a predetermined amount of compensation.

The presumption is that the compensation will incentivize the employee to work harder and achieve the goals. Typically, incentive compensation is not paid to employees for trying hard or for almost meeting the goal, but the employee is entitled to the agreed compensation when the goal is met. So with incentive compensation there is an *a priori* contractual agreement and an expectation that the employee's behavior will be influenced. Likewise, the employee expects compensation when they meet the goal.

A bonus is a contractual agreement that allows the employee to share in the "profits" of the company.

Although the amount is usually pre-determined and agreed upon, there is no expectation that the bonus program will influence the employee's specific behavior (drive, motivation, etc.). Nevertheless, both the employer and the employee feel good when the bonus program pays out, and they all feel part of the team. As is the case with an incentive, if the company does well, the employee feels entitled to the bonus. So a bonus is similar to an incentive, but there is no expectation of influencing the employee's behavior.

A reward has no *a priori* contractual agreement, so there is no expectation of influencing the employee's behavior.

Nevertheless, after the fact the employer offers the employee(s) some compensation for a job well done – examples include completing a project, finishing the year with a bang or achieving superior business results. In this situation, the employee has no expectation and is pleased by their employer's generosity.

To drive home the distinction between the three, let me highlight a subtle point.

When an incentive is paid out, the employer thanks the employee. When a reward is paid out, the employee thanks the employer. When a bonus is paid out, they both thank each other.

What works best: incentives, bonuses or rewards?

Do incentives work? Do they influence people's behaviors? Are people motivated enough by money that their behavior changes? The PBS article mentioned above has some interesting insight into these questions. Is there value to a bonus? If it's not intended to change behavior, why create the sense of entitlement? Do rewards have long-term value, or are they forgotten the next week? Do you have to reward everybody? Do you have to reward every year? If you do, do the incentives become an entitlement and degenerate into a bonus?

These are all questions you should ask yourself. You should have clear convictions and expectations in setting up a variable compensation program. Leading with intention is key. And, at a minimum, having clarity of intent and purpose creates intentionality.

Employee Incentives or Rewards – What Serves Customers Best?

June 2012

It's generally accepted that attractive incentives with clear goals motivate employees to achieve those goals. A telling example is the cash commission given to salespeople for achieving certain sales targets. Arguably, this is taken to the extreme with commissioned salespeople in car dealerships. How was your last car buying experience at a dealership? How much trust did you place in your salesperson? Were you wondering whose side they were on? Even if it is simply a perception, the words "car salesman" bring less than kind images to mind. Does it have to be that way?

Imagine walking into a dealership where the salespeople are not on commission, where they are more interested in your family and its needs than in filling their monthly quota. Imagine a dealership that has sold cars to your family and friends for years without anyone earning a direct commission on those sales. Well, welcome to Terry Ortynsky's Royal Ford in Yorkton, Saskatchewan.

Terry believes that commissioned salespeople find themselves in a conflict of interest with their duty to serve their customers.

To keep everybody focused on their tasks, dealerships often divide up their functions into sales/credit/lease or service/parts/body shop and have different departments run those functions with individual incentives. If your motto is to "Make it easy (for the customer)," as Terry's is, dividing up your dealership functions makes buying or servicing a vehicle more difficult for the customer. Yet, highly incentivized sales puts such an emphasis on closing the deal; the salesperson doesn't operate in the interest of the dealership or the customer. Terry believes the customer is better served by not having commissioned salespeople but, rather, competitively salaried employees receiving reasonable rewards when the company does well. At his dealership, he doesn't have compartmentalized functional departments or commissioned salespeople.

So what's the difference between incentives and "reasonable rewards?" Well, incentives are payments of cash or kind made by an employer to the employee when certain goals and metrics are achieved – as laid out in an implicit or explicit contract. In contrast, rewards are payments of cash or kind made by an employer to an employee *in appreciation* of achieving certain goals and metrics – totally at the discretion of the employer. In other words, incentives are intended to motivate the employee; rewards are a way of saying thank you to the employee.

What serves the customer better: incentives or rewards?

When designing incentives for your employees, make sure they aren't in conflict with your customers' interests. If they appear to be in conflict, both you and the customer might be better served by offering your employees rewards instead. Make your intention of rewarding them explicit, but do not enter into a contract on how and when the reward will occur.

As an epilogue to the story, I should point out that Terry Ortynsky's Royal Ford has served the Yorkton community for 25 years. And they think of their customers as family.

They have built a lifestyle-based culture within their company where the lifestyle is that of the dealership family. Imagine you were an employee of this company. What is your response going to be when your next-door neighbor asks you about your work at a backyard barbecue? Aren't you going to be proud of your dealership family? Maybe you'll even mention how your non-commissioned salespeople serve your customers better. Terry Ortynsky's Royal Ford has a lifestyle-based culture. But more importantly, it has an intentional culture.

Spot Awards: Their Use, Misuse and Abuse

February 2012

Most leaders appreciate the value of encouraging their employees, and companies adopt a variety of recognition tools to do so. This month, I want to discuss the values of a technique called Spot Awards and explore how they should be used, how companies often misuse them and how unlikely it is that the employees abuse them.

The concept of a Spot Award is to recognize an employee on the spot for their commendable behavior.

The recognition is usually in the form of a **token gift**, like a small gift card. Many companies adopt this practice, but most companies restrict its implementation in one of two ways, which significantly diminishes its value. They either place restrictions on who can award employees (usually managers) or they require that the awards be recommended to an approver who then approves the award, taking all of the empowerment out of the concept.

So here are my recommendations for implementing Spot Awards.

Determine a nominal value and form of the award.

Traditionally, I've used $50 gift certificates available at the desk of someone in administration. Announce to the whole company that any employee can make a Spot Award to any other employee, at any time, for any reason. Impose just two simple requirements for the sake of transparency and immediacy. Keep it transparent by asking the person recognizing the employee to provide a quotation to be published in the company newsletter when they collect the award. To keep it immediate, require that the award be given on the spot and presented to the recipient publicly, allowing everyone nearby to celebrate.

Will employees abuse this privilege?

My experience has been quite the contrary. In fact, the transparency of the award causes employees to take the responsibility very seriously. Most employees wish to demonstrate such high standards that they are reluctant to award it for anything less than extraordinary. "After all," they think, "My name is going in the company newsletter because I made the award!"

An award encourages three different parties: The onlookers who feel encouraged by a good deed being recognized, the recipient who is obviously pleased by the recognition and, most importantly, the person giving the award, who feels pride in encouraging a co-worker. When that person is empowered to give the award, they stand tall in recognizing the recipient. And this last and most useful value is lost when management imposes approvals and authorizations.

Even if Spot Awards were abused, what would be the cost?

An occasional frivolous award costs very little. And if there's collusion involved, you have a much bigger problem with those employees than the cost of a few gift certificates.

Recently, Julie Thorne Engels, senior vice president of creative design and strategy at The Regan Group in Hawthorne, CA, implemented Spot Awards within her marketing department as **YTB (You're the Best) Awards**. She said of her experience, "It's interesting that the team is really reserving this recognition for special moments that are above and beyond the call of duty. [It is] very exciting to witness [an employee's extraordinary contribution] and then watch the team applaud her efforts and excellence. [This demonstrates how the employees have taken] full accountability." Julie emphasizes that her team members "Fully respect the sanctity of the recognition, and reserve its use for truly deserving teammates."

Let Your Employees Dole Out the Bonuses

January 2010

This month's topic is a befitting start to the new year – a time when many companies plan their variable compensation programs. And it might be of particular interest to smaller companies or small divisions of larger companies. Mike Lieberman, CEO of Square 2 Marketing, gets credit for triggering this idea while we were discussing a similar topic.

Variable compensation is intended to motivate employees and align their interests with the interests of the company's owners.

The pool of money available to share with the employees is usually determined by the company's success. The available pool of money is distributed to the employees based on a combination of their responsibilities and their performance. In other words, devoid of performance consideration, higher-level employees will receive larger sums than lower-level employees. Top management then adjusts to reflect employee performance. Employees seldom understand the rationale behind the distribution. They usually resign themselves to what they see as a reality of life – management will get more whether or not they do a good job, and the worker-bees will get less no matter what.

So why not empower the employees to dole out the available pool of money?

Employees would give the CEO their recommendations on who should be rewarded and how much they should receive along with justifications for their recommendations. Each employee can recommend any set of employees in the company other than themselves. To keep these recommendations constrained, each employee is allowed to dole out as much money as they would have received from the pool devoid of performance considerations. So if the available pool of money, distributed without regard to employee performance, would have delivered Manager A $4,000 and Worker B $300, then Manager A gets to dole out $4,000 and worker B gets to dole out $300. This way, the CEO receives recommendations for precisely the amount of money available in the pool. Note that the pool remains the same size. The main difference is that employees are doling out the money rather than management. And the distribution is still performance based – as determined by peers, not management.

How will this motivate employees?

First, it empowers them to reward those who are deserving. It's been my experience that, for the most part, when these responsibilities are placed on employees, they take it seriously. Fully knowing the CEO is going to review their recommendations, employees put thought into their recommendations. Furthermore, it forces employees to understand, recognize and appreciate their colleagues' contributions.

The cynical manager might lament that lower level workers, being greater in number, will distribute all of the money among themselves, neither appreciating nor rewarding management for all their stress and responsibilities. The cynic should note that the amount of money lower level workers have to dole out is exactly equal to what they should collectively receive.

Obviously, the CEO can put some precautions in place. For example, the CEO might use this method to distribute only half the available funds, holding the other half to be distributed through more traditional top-down means. The CEO might reserve the right to veto errant recommendations that violate certain fundamental principles of ethics and company policy. But it's also important to preserve the integrity of the employees' recommendations to instill a true sense of empowerment. After all, this exercise is meant to help you hear your employees and help your employees feel heard. You might be pleasantly surprised by what an empowered workforce has to say.

Learnings of a Company That Let Its Employees Dole Out the Bonuses

May 2010

I have tossed around an idea to *Let Your Employees Dole Out the Bonuses* (See page 80). One company, Preferred Medical Marketing Corporation (PMMC) in Charlotte, NC, tried it themselves. This month's topic is a discussion of what they learned. Credit and thanks go to Roger Shaul, CEO of PMMC.

Roger, wanting to share some of 2009's profits with his employees in early 2010, divided the available pool of money in the ratio of his employees' base salaries and invited the employees to give away that amount to one or more deserving co-workers.

The employees were to submit their recommendations to Roger along with explanations of their choices.

Overall, the employees took the task seriously. Barring a couple of recommendations that peanut buttered awards to all employees, most employees took the time to understand and recognize specific contributions of a select number of co-workers. Roger received some very appreciative comments from people at the top and lower end because of the awards they received. Plus, he never had to exercise his veto over any errant recommendations. All of this demonstrates that when you place responsibilities on your employees, they take them seriously and follow through in earnest.

Who got recognized? Did the deserving get rewarded?

Roger found it understandable that some employees whose jobs entail serving other employees received a disproportionate amount of recognition and award. On the other hand, he was pleasantly surprised that certain lower level employees – whom management doesn't notice as much – got an unexpected amount of recognition and award from their peers. Roger says, "They were noted for their diligence, and they happen to have been very helpful to many outside their immediate department – real team players who care and are now obviously worthy of more appreciation and cultivation for advancement."

Another discovery Roger shared is that it's telling when certain people receive numerous awards and when others do not. Roger believes that there was some controversy in how the names were announced, and he received some complaints that choosing recipients was a task better left to management, but it died down very fast. By all accounts, Roger's experience seems to have been positive.

Would Roger do this again?

"The answer is a bit complex," Roger notes. "The awards were given because the company did not make salary adjustments during the previous year. The company did better than expected during the recession, and it seemed appropriate because of management's commitment to offer rewards if we did well. Bottom line: if the company does better than expected next year, yes, and we should. What would we do differently? I believe it may be prudent to leave management off the list of recipients but perhaps still on the list of those who grant the awards."

Focus of Executive Compensation: When, Not How Much

April 2009

Last month, when the world was in uproar over the bonuses paid out to AIG executives, this topic seemed timely. But now that public scrutiny has shifted to the auto industry bailout and the world economic summit, this topic might seem a little passé. Nevertheless, I think it merits attention because I often talk about *how much* compensation executives are paid but not *when they deserve* to get paid.

The inspiration for this idea came from the Inverted Bonus Plan implemented at Planar Systems almost a decade ago. The premise is that CEOs and other top corporate executives are, by selection, desirous of making money. While there needs to be some focus on how much they get paid, far more attention needs to focus on when they are deemed to have earned their pay. Executives of a corporation – especially a public corporation – have a stewardship responsibility to ensure that those with less influence on the results of the corporation and a vested interest in those results are fully served before they serve themselves. Often, this important principle isn't demanded or nurtured by public company boards.

Take, for example, the defense offered by many of the AIG executives justifying their bonus payments. "We were not in that division when it collapsed," they say. "We were asked to come in and clean up," they explain. Their comments show a lack of the stewardship principle. Those executives, like senior AIG executives in other parts of the company, had a responsibility to the shareholders and lower level employees to ensure that the assets of the corporation were not squandered. It's their failure to execute their stewardship responsibility that makes their bonus pay so outrageous independent of where they were in the division at the time of the collapse.

The public is not outraged that some corporate executives get millions of dollars in bonuses; it's that AIG executives received any kind of bonus this year. The public is happy to pay a princely sum of money to executives of successful corporations who deliver on their stewardship responsibility, but this is only true if bonuses are withheld when executives fail to do so. So the issue isn't really how much they have earned but when they have earned it.

Don't Let Your CEO Take the Money and Run

October 2008

You can probably tell by the title that this month's topic is inspired by the financial crisis on Wall Street, its spillover into foreign markets and the ensuing legislative actions being taken by governments. Needless to say, the general public and legislators alike aren't too thrilled about the large sums of money senior executives of failed financial institutions are walking away with. The $700 billion bailout plan enacted by the United States Congress last week will certainly cap executive compensation – at least for institutions that take advantage of the bailout.

Do CEOs always get to walk away with excessive compensation after doing such a poor job? Or is this just a phenomenon of greedy Wall Street fat cats who are tempted to take huge risks for hefty personal gains and, in the process, end up destroying their companies' balance sheets? Can boards of smaller companies take comfort in the fact they don't pay their CEOs tens of millions of dollars? Or should even small- to mid-cap public companies get ahead of the curve and ensure that CEOs don't walk away with a large bonus one year and get thrown out of the job the next?

What if boards adopted a policy where, even when duly earned, large cash compensation (each company would have to define "large") isn't paid out until the company's financials withstand the test of time? For example, a company might decide that the CEO, though eligible to earn more than a million dollars of compensation in a year, will not be paid more than a million dollars in that year. The excess will be held by the company and paid at the end of three years, much like a forced deferred compensation, with the caveat that the board has specific authority to withhold that payment for specified reasons.

I realize this idea opens up a rat's nest of issues, not the least of which is specifying the reasons for withholding payment. One can only imagine the welcome sign hung on the door for all the lawyers downtown. While recognizing the idea needs significant sharpening, I maintain that all public companies – small and large – in all industries, not just the financial sector, need to proactively take steps to ensure their CEO doesn't take the money and run. If you don't come up with ideas, the government will!

Why Severance Pay? Why Not Retention Pay?

July 2007

Severance pay, a customary clause in executives' employment contracts, was probably designed to ensure financial security for executives. However, when it comes to CEOs of public companies, most of whom are financially secure, companies use severance pay commitments to stay market competitive. In other words, a board would have difficulty recruiting a high-quality CEO without offering severance pay.

I'd like to propose an alternative to severance pay called retention pay, which offers comparable market competitiveness but is more shareholder-friendly. As the name suggests, retention pay is meant to retain the executive for another year in lieu of severance payment upon termination.

Here is how retention pay might work.

Let's say that traditional, market competitive severance pay would equal twice the annual salary. Let's also assume the average tenure of a CEO is four years. Under these assumptions, the proposed retention pay arrangement would guarantee the CEO a retention pay of one-half the annual salary for each year the board retains them. The board would have to decide on an annual basis whether they want the CEO to serve in that role for an additional year. Should they choose to retain the CEO, they are obligated to make the retention payment in addition to all other customary compensation items. The retention payment might be paid in four quarterly installments to ensure that the CEO serves through the year to collect the amount. However, if the board chooses not to retain the CEO for another year, they may terminate the CEO without cause and without any severance obligations.

If the CEO's tenure, as determined through the board's annual decisions, is exactly four years (the assumed average for CEOs) then the CEO would receive four retention payments, which is comparable to the severance pay they would have otherwise received. If the tenure is longer, the CEO comes out ahead – as it should be. If the tenure is shorter, the CEO comes out behind – as it should be – providing a better alignment with shareholder interests.

At first sight, this might seem like an egregious payment to CEOs who are already being paid handsomely in cash and equity compensation. But observe that there is no new money involved in this proposal. You are simply paying the expected value of severance payments in the form of retention payments, using the same money to reward a CEO's good performance that you would have paid for an unacceptable performance.

There are a number of other advantages to this approach.

The board has to overtly decide every year to make a substantial payment for retaining the executive. The board is less likely to tolerate another year with an under-performing CEO when it has to "pay to keep" but is "free to let go." In CEO recruitment, retention pay – as a substitute to severance pay – should be more appealing to self-confident CEOs who think they can outlast the average tenure. Additionally, the accounting becomes cleaner and represents the true compensation costs. Instead of having a large "one-time, non-recurring" severance cost every four years or so, retention pay can be accounted for on an ongoing basis, every quarter, reflecting the true cost of doing business.

There are a number of questions to be answered:

What about equity considerations in severance? Why should a voluntarily departing CEO get a windfall of the retention pay already paid? Is retention pay paid the very first year of appointment? How does retention pay impact change-in-control arrangements? Can retention pay be held by the company as deferred pay until termination? If so, is it then identical to severance pay? For the sake of brevity, I won't elaborate on these and other questions. Suffice it to say, just thinking through this provocative approach might be beneficial for a board that's in the process of recruiting a new CEO.

Should Most Employees Receive Stock Options?

November 2007

The idea for this month's *Food for Thought* came out of an interview with Google's director of compensation, Dave Rolefson. Recognizing that employees often do not appreciate the full value of a stock option, Google created an active market for vested employee stock options. Google employees can log in to their account and observe the current marketable value of their vested options in real time. And they can choose to sell those option contracts. The market – consisting of employee sellers and institutional buyers – offers a value for the option that is clearly more than the difference between strike and market price – though slightly lower than the Black-Scholes value. This has allowed Google to clearly communicate to its employees the full value of the options they hold.

That got me to thinking whether employees in most companies really understand the true value of stock options.

During the high-tech boom of the '80s and '90s, many companies began to use employee stock options as a broad-based compensation tool for most, if not all, employees. The belief was that employee stock options allowed the company to align the interests of employees with the interests of shareholders. Executives recognized that not all employees could easily see the link between what they do and how the stock price moves. Nevertheless, in a bullish market there was considerable appeal in using a non-cash compensation tool like stock options – particularly when it didn't have an impact on the company's net income.

The party ended in 2005 with the pronouncement of Financial Accounting Standards123(R), which required public companies in the U.S. to take an accounting charge to their income statement representing the value of the employee stock options that vested during the period of the statement. So, many companies have begun asking if the broad-based use of stock options is meaningful and worth the accounting charge it entails. How should a company answer that question?

I have a provocative proposal inspired by Google's approach.

Imagine if an employee who was to receive an option grant were offered a choice to either accept the grant under its vesting terms or receive a cash award equivalent to the Black-Scholes value of the option grant, keeping in mind the cash payment is also subject to the same vesting terms as the options. If the employee were inclined to choose the cash award, then an option award would be an ineffective use of company resources. The company might as well have retained more value by offering a cash grant. Cash-strapped companies aside, one should not delude themselves into thinking that a cash grant constitutes real money and an option grant does not. The company is simply using the shareholders' money!

If the choice between a cash grant and an option grant is offered to all employees receiving stock option grants, and if a predominance of those employees choose the cash grant (which is more than likely with most companies), then the company needs to rethink its stock option policy.

For example, a company might satisfy (or more than satisfy) its employees by offering a cash award at a discount to the Black-Scholes value. Clearly, there is some discounted value – say, 60 percent of the Black-Scholes value, for the sake of a concrete conversation – where there's an even split within the employee group between a cash award and an option award. The company might be able to offer that choice and save 40 percent of its cost for half the employees. It could be argued that the discounted value that splits the employee group evenly represents the true value of the options. U.S. Securities and Exchange Commission (SEC) permitting, the company might consider using the discounted value, in place of the Black Scholes valuation, to record their expense for the options. This is somewhat similar to the approach – albeit an open market approach – used by Zions Bancorporation and Cisco that won SEC approval.

Lastly, a company that offers this choice to its employees can use the trend data from year-to-year as an indicator of employee confidence in management's ability to create shareholder value. While the risk profile and personal situations of individual employees are bound to impact the data in any given year, the trend data from year-to-year is likely to factor that out. Do I dare ask if a public company that offers this choice should publish the trend data to its investing public?

Just in case someone mistakenly concludes that using restricted stock instead of options is a similar concept, let me point out that providing a choice to the employees is the key component that creates an active market.

I recognize that this approach, while providing comparable retention value, ignores the value of aligning the interests of the employees with those of the shareholders – a much-touted feature of stock options. But in reality, it is questionable if the behavior of lower level employees is significantly altered through stock options (at least beyond what profit-sharing-style compensation tools enable). There's no doubt that stock options serve as an alignment tool for executives, but this approach might serve as a more cost-effective alternative to broad-based use of stock options.

Should Stock Options Be Viewed as Pay Increases?

March 2007

This month, I want to explore a new way of looking at stock options: as an increase in the targeted variable pay for the recipient.

This is not about expensing options or even about whether they should be expensed. Rather, this is about how management should view the award of options while expecting performance from the recipient. Should management view an employee with a large number of vested, in-the-money options as more expensive to the shareholder, expecting a greater level of contributions to the company than an employee without those options? Should management take those options into account when it comes time for their performance evaluation, treating them like an employee at a higher pay level? More poignantly, if the company decides to reduce its workforce, should an employee with a greater number of options be viewed as more expensive?

Performance Management

The most common topic of these articles has been performance management. Of all the ideas suggested in these articles, the most used and implemented idea is the Levels of Performance. This simple concept has found considerable appeal. I really enjoyed writing the article, "Mediocrity Invited." It was probably because of its departure from my usual scholarly style to a satirical style. That article forms the basis of this chapter.

The Parking Lot Exercise has been a keystone of my executive management. I have used it in the companies I have run. And while it might seem harsh, I contend that it is more compassionate than the pretense of sugar-coated messages that most managers send.

Performance management is probably the hardest thing for most management and executives. The problem with performance management is that most executives view this as a problem of the employee. Yet when confronted with framing the situation as, "within the circumstances in which the employee is required to perform, the employee has been unable to perform," the executive realizes the two-way street called performance management. Is the employee not performing because we have not enabled them to perform or are they just not capable of performing?

Hiring, growing, retaining and developing are probably the biggest tasks of management. I hope these articles spark some ideas.

Mediocrity Invited

July 2015

In most of our companies, we have a big sign with bold letters over the main door into our building. It has been there a long time and is such a regular part of the fixtures that we have lost sight of it. Although we diligently practice what the sign says, few of us, if any, notice it as we walk in and out of the building each day. We probably can't even remember what it says, so let me remind you: "Mediocrity Invited."

We do many things to ensure that mediocre employees feel totally safe and secure and are not made uncomfortable. This month's article illustrates examples of things we do to ensure that we stay true to the promise on that sign.

Accountability is uncomfortable, so ignore it.

Most companies have difficulty creating a culture of holding people accountable. When somebody has not done an action item from the previous meeting, we merely note it and move on. Holding that individual accountable on the spot is uncomfortable – for ourselves and the delinquent. So instead, we don't hold them accountable. By the way, who in your company would prefer that you hold people accountable? Obviously, the ones who are accountable. Who would not prefer it? The people who aren't accountable, of course! Oh yes, I forgot the signage on the front door. We wouldn't want to make the unaccountable uncomfortable, would we?

Put off performance management a little longer.

Most managers who have let go of an employee will confess, when asked, that they waited too long to take action. At the same time, they acknowledge that the peers of the non-performing employee had noticed the lack of performance long before the manager even became aware of it, much less took action on it. So the performing employees, who have picked up the non-performer's slack, have been waiting patiently for management to take action. Ask yourself, who in your company would like management to take quick action on non-performing employees? The performing ones. Who would prefer that you be cautious, deliberate and slow in taking action? I suppose the non-performing ones. Oh yes, the signage on the front door! Never mind.

Don't celebrate one person if it's going to ruffle others.

We all like to recognize employees for good deeds done, particularly deeds that are beyond the call of duty. We want to acknowledge them publicly, but fear its impact on somebody left out. The fear of giving recognition is the fear of upsetting those unrecognized. So we include a few more people in the recognition.

The other day one of the senior managers came back from a great industry gathering where our advertising work was featured prominently and received a lot of accolades. True to our culture of celebrating success, he sent out a company-wide email sharing the joy and recognizing a half a dozen people. Just in case he had missed a few others who might have contributed, he added a caveat that he was rushed in sending the email and promised to send another with any names he may have missed. And yet, I suspect that there were probably one or two individuals who really stood out in making that advertising campaign a success. Would we be comfortable pointing out just one person? Of course not. Instead, we dilute that recognition by including everyone.

In many companies where management recognizes individuals at their monthly all-hands meetings, executives work hard to ensure that everybody gets a turn to be recognized. They don't want one name called out too often and many names never called out at all. Who would prefer this approach? The people who would otherwise not be recognized. Oh, I forgot about the sign again. My apologies.

Pay over-performers and under-performers the same salary.

Recently, my director of HR sent a memo to the executive team asking for input on the annual salary review process that we will undertake in a few months. Compensation has been a frequent topic in these *Food for Thought* articles. Although most companies espouse "pay for performance," they practice "pay for pulse."

If you truly believe in paying for performance, ask yourself this: Does the spread of salaries among comparable employees resemble anything close to the spread of their individual performances?

Most managers will admit that high performing employees contribute several times the amount that poorly performing employees do. Yet is the star performer paid double or triple the salary of a poor performer? It's tough to spread the salaries of poor and high performing employees through meager annual salary increases. So how can we spread the salaries to reflect their relative performance? Here's a collection of ideas, though I admit most of them are bizarre, and I'll conclude with the only practical idea I have actually used.

Option 1: Guarantee a raise or resignation

What would happen if you announced to your employees that you were abandoning the practice of annual salary reviews and corresponding salary adjustments? From here on out, you will practice a flat salary model unless the employee requests a salary review. Tell your employees: "If you want a salary increase, just come and ask. All you have to do is ask! All I require is that you bring your resignation with you. I will guarantee one of the two. Just come and ask. Come anytime. Come often!"

What kind of employees in your company would like this approach? The high performing, confident ones. Who would fear this approach? The non-performing employees who lack confidence. So why won't we do this? The signage on the front door. That's why.

Option 2: Take from poor performers to reward high performers

Annual salary increases usually average a small percentage increase, say three or four percent, reflecting movement in the market and the company's financial appetite. That small a number leaves little room to really recognize the high performer with a distinctly higher salary.

That leads us to our next bizarre idea. What if you had all employees, upon employment, sign an understanding that the offered salary is for the remainder of the calendar year? At the beginning of each year, every employee's salary will be automatically reduced by 10 percent. Furthermore, indicate in the agreement that you commit to contribute the 10 percent savings from the entire payroll to the pool of money available for annual salary increases. So now each year an employee's average salary increase can be 13 or 14 percent! Of course, you intend to reach that average by distributing much larger percentages to the high performers and very low percentages to the poor performers. Again, who would like or dislike this idea? It's too bad about that sign.

Option 3: No increases below five percent

Finally, here's something more practical, and something I've at least tried out myself. When management conducts salary reviews and plans out annual salary increases for each employee, they are always cognizant of the total payroll impact. It's usually measured in terms of the (weighted) average of all of the salary increases given to the entire workforce. Seldom if ever does management examine the standard deviation of that distribution. Would you prefer a high standard deviation or a low figure? A high figure indicates a wide spread in the increases – some employees (hopefully performing ones) receiving large increases and others (hopefully non-performing ones) receiving low increases. You would want a wide spread.

How do you get a high standard deviation, yet keep the mean at the, say, 3.7 percent you have budgeted? Well, you have to give a lot of zero increases to afford a 15 percent increase for your star performers. How can you achieve that? It's really quite easy. Require your management to achieve the 3.7 percent average with the caveat that nobody can be granted an increase between the amounts of zero and five percent. So all the increases have to be either zero or five percent and above. Yet the average must compute to 3.7 percent. You will get your desired result. Tempting as it is, I will not ask the question of who would like this approach and remind you of the sign. But I guess I just did.

Next time you enter the front door of your building, take a look at that sign. How long has it been up there? Who takes note of it? How have those words worked their way into your company's practices? If you want to replace that signage with something beneficial, here is a suggestion. Put up a real sign over the door that reads, "The sign that used to hang here has been intentionally removed." It should persuade your employees to come and ask you what the new signage means. You will be intentionally causing a conversation.

The Gallery Owner's Dilemma

June 2010

Credit for this topic goes to my friend and colleague Steve Buhaly who recently reminded me of the gallery owner's dilemma.

Imagine you wanted to open an art gallery.

You scout out some good commercial venues for the gallery, choose a place and sign a lease. You know the type and amount of wall space available at the gallery. You travel through art auctions and buy just the right kind of art to attract the clientele you want. You buy just the right amount of artwork to fill the gallery while giving it that spacious, aesthetic appeal. Then, with all of the artwork beautifully displayed, you open the doors and customers begin to pour in.

Some of your art pieces sell very quickly, creating holes in the walls, so you go to the auction and buy more artwork to fill in the holes. Though most of your selections seem to be popular with your clientele, you occasionally make mistakes, buying pieces every so often that don't seem to sell. Nevertheless, other pieces sell and you keep filling in the holes. After a couple of years of doing this, what do you have on your walls? All the artwork that nobody wants!

Obviously, a smart gallery owner knows that stagnant artwork has to be discounted and moved. Otherwise, the gallery will become unattractive.

Now imagine starting a department in your business or your company.

You hire a group of people that you thought could do the job and let them go at it. Some of them do well. They get promoted. Some do well and move on to other jobs in other departments or companies. As people move on, you hire new people to fill in the vacancies. After a couple of years, who do you have filling up your department? All the people that nobody else wants!

What are you doing about the gallery owner's dilemma? Are you finding ways to "discount and move out" the non-performers?

Are Some of Your Employees in the Parking Lot?

July 2010

I have previously described *The Gallery Owner's Dilemma* (See page 98) and observed that a gallery is likely to be full of unwanted artwork if the owner doesn't take active steps to move it out when it doesn't sell. Likewise, I observed that managers would get stuck with unwanted people if they didn't take active steps to move them out. So what options do the managers have?

Here's a provocative option. It's called the Parking Lot Exercise.

Let's say you're a manager with 10 people reporting to you. Imagine you could let your entire team go but keep them in the parking lot. Imagine that, just as magically, you had recruiting efforts underway for the 10 open positions and you've received numerous applications, including 10 from your colleagues in the parking lot. Which of the 10 would you hire back from the parking lot? What should you do with the remaining colleagues still standing in the parking lot, waiting for this fun thought experiment to end? You had better do something! In essence, you've just decided that if you were to reconstitute your team, it would not include those people left in the parking lot.

Here's what you do: Have a candid conversation with each of them.

Tell them that you conducted this thought experiment and they were left standing in the parking lot. Tell them how you arrived at that conclusion and explain what they need to do to stay out of the parking lot the next time. Emphasize the fact that you are NOT firing the individual, but make it clear that if you were to reconstitute your team, they wouldn't be on it.

Is this brutal or compassionate?

If I assume correctly that there are members of your team in the parking lot, isn't it in everybody's interest that they know? "I would have communicated that during the performance review," you argue. How many performance reviews clearly communicate to the employee, in some way, that they are in the parking lot?

This practice was implemented in a 500-1000 employee company for five years, during which time its revenue grew from $100 million to $250 million.

All employees were subjected to it, including the CEO. During every annual performance review, each manager was required to communicate to their employees whether the employee was in the parking lot with a clear yea/nay response. Even the board of directors communicated the same to the CEO. During those five years, there were, at any instant, between 18 percent and 22 percent of employees in the parking lot – figuratively speaking. In addition to being on a performance improvement plan, employees in the parking lot were ineligible to receive stock options. Almost all involved found the exercise to be an honest practice – even if brutally honest at times.

The Parking Lot Exercise provides clarity and puts a level of responsibility on both the manager and the employee. Clearly, the employee has been forewarned, but the manager also takes on the responsibility of addressing the issue with a clear time frame. Essentially, the manager talking to the employee is like the gallery owner putting a yellow sticky note on the back of the artwork, reminding the owner when the artwork should be discounted or scrapped.

Levels of Performance

March 2011

Naturally, performance management tends to focus predominantly on non-performers. I'm not suggesting that you need to manage the performance of the high performers, but what about the ones who are good performers but not as good as you thought they were?

Have you ever heard of Aristotle's Law of the Excluded Middle? Human beings seem to harbor the assumption that something is exclusively right or wrong, good or bad. An employee is either a good performer or a bad performer, right? The fact is that there is a large middle ground between somebody who is a good performer (i.e. somebody you wish to have on your team) and somebody who is a bad performer (i.e. somebody you would rather let go).

To better explain this concept, here's a new approach to assessing an employee's level of performance.

An employee is said to be performing at a "selectable" level of performance if their level of performance is such that, should their position become vacant and that employee be available in the market, knowing all you know about that employee, you would voluntarily select that individual to fill that position.

An employee is said to be performing at an "incumbent" level of performance if their level of performance is such that, should their position become vacant and that employee be available in the market, knowing all you know about that employee, you would NOT voluntarily select that employee for that position. But given that that employee currently occupies that position, and there is a cost associated with getting rid of that employee and additional costs associated with hiring a new employee, training that new employee, etc., and taking into account the probability that the newly hired employee is going to be any better than your current employee, you conclude that it is not in your economic interest to let go of your current employee. In other words, the current employee maintains their position only because they are the incumbent.

Finally, an employee is said to be performing at an **"unacceptable" level of performance** if their level of performance is such that it's in your best interest to spend the time, energy and cost to get rid of that person and find somebody else.

Most performance management systems focus on employees at or near the unacceptable level of performance.

You should really begin the process the second they leave the selectable level and enter the incumbent level.

To illustrate this, consider a newly hired employee. By definition, your estimate of their anticipated level of performance is at a selectable level. If, at some future date – many months down the road maybe – they should end up at an unacceptable level of performance, they must have fallen through the incumbent level. So why wait until they reach the unacceptable level? Why not catch them as they move from the selectable level to the incumbent level?

If you accept that idea, you should be willing to have a candid conversation with an employee who just entered the incumbent level of performance – the employee whose departure is not in your economic interest. Let that employee know that, should you reconstitute your team, you would not voluntarily hire that person. I called this tool the Parking Lot Exercise in my previous post, *Are Some of Your Employees in the Parking Lot?* (See page 99.)

By having the conversation, you can accomplish one of two outcomes: either the employee realizes the gravity of the situation and makes changes, or you shorten the time initially set out for the employee to move from the incumbent phase to the unacceptable phase.

Are you willing to have that conversation?

Unfortunately, most managers avoid that conversation because they fear the employee will look for another job and leave. "After all," the manager argues, "it's not in my economic interest to lose that employee!" As a result, these managers tolerate an employee that they wouldn't voluntarily hire into that position. What kind of alternative is that?

Mind those Q's

August 2014

In February of 2014, Tom Friedman, a *New York Times* columnist, wrote an article on how the hiring practices at Google have changed from focusing on GPAs and graduates from prestigious schools to a broader index of indicators. That inspired me to formalize an informal framework for hiring that I have been putting to use.

Would you like to hire intelligent people?

For most professional jobs, the answer is likely to be yes, but what is intelligence? There are hundreds of definitions, and the one I offer here is probably consistent with most of them: Intelligence is the ability to observe, comprehend, abstract, reason and then deduce conclusions. Intelligence is often measured by a series of tests resulting in an intelligence quotient or IQ. However, these tests unduly emphasize the manipulation of data and facts and place little emphasis on the observation of one's surroundings. Howard Gardner advanced the theory of multiple intelligences, and Daniel Goleman popularized the concept of emotional intelligence. EQ became the informal moniker to capture one's emotional intelligence, a person's capacity to "observe, comprehend, abstract, reason and deduce conclusions" from the emotions of people around them.

So should we focus on both IQ and EQ? Hold your horses! I want to offer you many more Q's!

In addition to IQ and EQ, I suggest you consider eight other Q's, informal measures of eight attributes, when looking for a suitable individual for a specific role – be it an employee, a friend, a sports teammate, etc. Along with a definition for each quotient, I want to offer a framework for thinking about them. I'll also dive into a very unique Q that I chose to leave off the list.

IQ and EQ measure intelligence – the ability to observe, comprehend, abstract, reason and deduce conclusions from structured information or human emotions. These attributes are inherent to the individual and the power of their mind, and they're likely to exhibit these attributes in any situation they find themselves in.

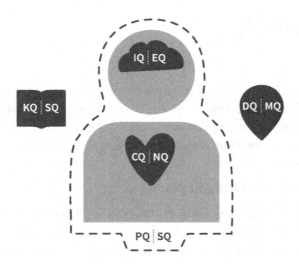

KQ and SQ, standing for **Knowledge Quotient** and **Skills Quotient**, provide a measure of the individual's knowledge and skill in a relevant discipline. Knowledge is the amassing, retention and recollection of information, and skill is the expertise in doing specific tasks – usually attained through years of practice. Both KQ and SQ are specific to a discipline. They do not transfer from one discipline to another. They are subject matter specific.

DQ and MQ, standing for **Diligence Quotient** and **Motivation Quotient**, provide a measure of the individual's diligence and motivation in a particular situation. Observe that diligence is the individual's commitment to work hard, put the nose to the grindstone and get the job done. In contrast, motivation is the individual's drive to succeed, to accomplish and reach goals. Both of these attributes are situation dependent, although one might argue that a diligent individual is likely to be diligent in any situation. Nevertheless, I believe the situation has a significant bearing on the individual's diligence and motivation.

CQ and NQ, standing for **Character Quotient** and **Niceness Quotient** (kindness), provide a measure of the individual's ethics and kindness. Good character is about doing what is right. In contrast, kindness is about doing something nice. Both character and kindness are attributes of the individual and captures the individual's heart, so to speak. Like IQ and EQ, an individual is likely to exhibit these attributes in any situation.

Finally, PQ and SQ, standing for **Personality Quotient** and **Sociability Quotient**, provide a measure of how the individual interacts with others and how the individual presents themselves. Personality includes aspects of the individual's appearance, their behavior, mannerisms, charisma and the like. In contrast, sociability relates more to interactions with others (both one-on-one and in group settings), the individual's ability to collaborate and be a team player and, importantly, the individual's leadership capabilities. Again, PQ and SQ are attributes of the individual and are likely to be exhibited in all situations.

An obvious omission in the above Q's is a measure of one's creativity.

Is creativity an intrinsic attribute, separate from intelligence? Or does intelligence measure creativity? What is creativity, anyway? Is somebody who is creative in one discipline likely to be creative in another? Does the situation have a bearing? I believe creativity is a combination of intelligence, the discipline (subject matter) and the situation. For this reason, I've chosen to omit it as an independent attribute.

All that said, are all the Q's equal?

Are they all important? What I suggest is that you be intentional about which Q's are most important when evaluating individuals for a position. Then seek to understand how the individual stands up in each of those measures. Observe that when you seek others' input on the candidate, their comments on knowledge, sociability, diligence and motivation may or may not transfer. What attributes are likely to transfer are IQ, EQ, character, niceness, personality and sociability. So focus your own independent exploration on the former list and seek references to assess the latter list. Being intentional about the Q's allows you to mind the Q's efficiently.

Would You Tender Your Resignation?

June 2008

Imagine that your CEO sent out the following memo to every employee in the company:

Dear Fellow Employee,

I invite you to submit to me your resignation. Let me first say that you do not have to; it is not obligatory. And, should you choose not to do so, I assure you there will be no punitive consequences.

However, if you do submit your resignation and I choose not to accept it, I guarantee a 10 percent bonus on the spot. Mind you, if you submit your resignation and I do accept it, your resignation would be considered to have been tendered voluntarily, and as such you will not be entitled to any severance.

Have a wonderful day!

Your CEO

How would you react?

What would you do? What would the water cooler conversation be as soon as the memo went out?

If you are the head of the company or a leader in the company, I urge you to think about what those water cooler conversations would sound like. What percentage of the employees in your company do you think would tender their resignation? More importantly, would you accept them?

One Company's Experience With the Resignation Exercise

June 2011

In the article *Would You Tender Your Resignation?* I offered a provocative letter from a CEO inviting their employees to tender their resignation (See page 106). Although the letter might be unlawful in some, impractical in most and certainly difficult to execute in all jurisdictions, there is another way you can realize its potential. It's a hypothetical exercise I call **The Resignation Exercise**.

The idea is for the CEO to bring their executive team into a conference room and pretend – just pretend – that they had sent out that same resignation letter to their employees.

The executive team then discusses how each of the employees would react to the letter, who might submit their resignations and whose resignations they would accept. This discussion is intended to point out the employees in the parking lot, à la *Are Some of Your Employees in the Parking Lot?* (See page 99). This discussion, involving the full participation of the executive team, makes each executive think about their problem employees. My claim that "rational people acting intentionally always do the right thing" ensures that this hypothetical exercise will lead to appropriate actions by the executives.

Right now, you might be thinking that your company doesn't have employees whose resignations you would accept. Well, I also claim that almost all companies larger than a few people have employees whose resignation management would accept. In fact, most companies have employees (often called prima donnas) who have a false self-assessment of being indispensable.

Michael Easton, president and CEO of Argus Industries in Winnipeg, Manitoba, decided to go through with the resignation exercise.

He and his executive team spent half a day going over 52 employees, asking themselves, "Whose resignations should we accept?" After discussing each employee, they placed the employee's name on a four-point "Hero to Zero" chart.

- Hero

- Right Person – Right Seat

- Right Person – Wrong Seat

- Zero-Off the bus.

The executive team began to form an understanding of where each employee fits on the Argus "bus": key person, good person, someone to move to a new position or someone who needs to get off the bus.

What does Michael think of the exercise?

"We had a fantastic discussion about our people, where we needed to move them and just accepted that we couldn't keep protecting some staff who just really didn't cut it anymore. And we really had to work together to find a new place for employees who need to start adding value to the company again. We all thought it was very valuable and a great way to bring the team together and strategize about the future."

The moral of the story: Out of the box ideas, executed within the box of a conference room, can bring considerable value.

Where Is the Bottom Half?

March 2008

This topic is probably the most controversial item in my **"Internal Corporate Governance"** talk that I give to boards of public companies. One item in my 10-point recommendation deals with term limits for directors and chairmen of public company boards. I recommend that directors should remain associated with a board for no longer than three three-year terms, or about 10 years. The most common argument against this idea is that formulaic solutions are too simplistic for an issue as complex as directors receiving tenure.

My belief is based on the observation that half the directors of public companies are below the median among their peers.

It's fair to say that you probably don't want anybody from the bottom half in your boardroom. So who are they? As they say at the poker table, "If you don't know who the mark is, it's you!" Based on a similar observation about their employees – that half are below the median – many companies institute a systematic topgrading process. But those executive-style tools used to manage employee tenure are not as applicable to an elected board, which tries to operate with collegiality and consensus. The result is that directors are seldom asked to leave. And when they are, it's more likely to be for political reasons than performance reasons. That's why I contend that a formulaic approach provides a solution with net positive benefits.

While directors have reservations over term limits, the second half of my proposal – term limits for serving as chairman – is usually met with a warm reception. Most believe rotating the chair – say, every three years – allows for a change in dynamics within the boardroom while maintaining intellectual continuity among the directors. In any case, changing the cast of characters in a boardroom causes the board to be less content with the status quo.

Performing Employee Archetypes

October 2014

I have often discussed the cost of non-performing employees, and this month I want to discuss the potential costs of performing employees. What? There are potential costs, even when my employees are performing? Yes. And it all comes down to motivation. Even though an employee might be performing well, it's crucial that you understand the motivation that drives them to perform. Because, if you understand that motivation, you'll know why his or her performance might degrade, and you'll know how to address those situations. So how do you understand an employee's motivations?

I have come up with four archetypes of performing employees: Farmer, Hunter, Soldier and Terrorist.

The **Farmer** gets up every morning before the break of dawn to milk the cows and feed the animals. He toils all day tending to his crop and his herd. Like clockwork, he comes in at noon for his big mid-day meal, only to return to bale hay all afternoon. At dusk, he retires, tired from a long day's work. He does this day in and day out. He has little interest in anything but his farm – takes little note of the economy, politics or sports. He is solely focused on his work.

I am sure you know of employees of this archetype. They are steady, dependable and hardworking. But they are usually reluctant to take work home or work on the weekends unless absolutely necessary. They have minimal interests beyond their work, showing little interest in the company's performance, changes in the industry or emerging tools and techniques. They are unlikely to embrace change, adopt new practices or reinvent themselves. But for now, they are good, performing employees.

The **Hunter** likes the thrill of the kill. He works hard, perseveres, displays patience when needed and shows aggression when appropriate. He is focused on the prize, and the prize is what drives him. When he finally hunts down the animal, he hoists the beast onto his back so he can proudly display his accomplishment when he returns to camp.

Employees of this archetype are very focused on the goal. And when they achieve that goal, they expect to be rewarded – financially, emotionally and with status. They don't like egalitarian distribution of rewards. They believe in the strong surviving and the weak starving. The hunter wonders, "What does that mean for me?" when it comes to changes in compensation philosophies, assignment of duties, and organizational structure. They usually have large egos that need to be periodically stroked. But for now, they are performing employees who consistently deliver results.

The **Soldier**, like the hunter, works hard, perseveres and shows patience or aggression as needed. But unlike the hunter, the soldier works for a cause. The soldier is not looking for personal glory or wealth, but fulfillment of that cause.

To understand employees of this archetype, you must understand their cause. In my technology background, there were many situations where an employee's cause was a commitment to a particular technology. Non-profits are often filled with soldiers. But even in a for-profit corporation, you will find soldiers with a market-focused cause or a product-focused cause. For the soldier, winning is not about making money. Winning is about proving his point and serving the cause. When a corporation chooses to move the focus away from a soldier's cause, the soldier fights the organization tooth and nail. But, for now, the soldier is a well-performing, committed employee.

The **Terrorist** is like a soldier, but his cause is to eradicate a particular injustice he sees in his world. He believes that this injustice is being perpetrated by the powers-that-be, and he views himself as powerless to fight the establishment. He is so convinced of the injustice that he will abandon accepted norms of behavior to fight the establishment. The terrorist employee is usually someone with a unique skill set that you cannot do without. He knows his value to the organization and he discharges his duties diligently.

Examples of injustice that infuriate the terrorist employee include particular gripes with compensation, abhorrence of certain management practices and complaints of opportunities held from certain groups of employees. His unique expertise enables him to hold management hostage. But, for now, management tolerates his temper tantrums so that the unique tasks can get done.

In all four archetypes, the employees are competent, committed and performing their duties well.

But their behavior, both current and future, can lead to difficult situations. Management needs to understand each archetype, their motivation and possible changes in the business that could upset their motivation.

Additionally, certain cultures will find it difficult to accept certain archetypes.

In my Intentional Corporate Culture program, I ask clients to intentionally choose from four types of culture: loyalty-based, competition-based (sometimes called performance-based), opportunity-based and lifestyle-based. Hunters will find it difficult to operate in a loyalty-based culture, while farmers will experience similar difficulties in a competition-based culture, and terrorists will be unwelcome in an opportunity-based culture. Being intentional about the style of your culture will enable you to be more selective when hiring new people and more deliberate in nurturing your employees.

I've offered four archetypes of performing employees, but there might be more.

My experience has shown that, in most cases, you can understand your employees as one of these archetypes. My intent is not to suggest that one type is better than the other; even the terrorist has a legitimate role to play – he just feels downtrodden. Understanding the archetype of each performing employee allows management to be intentional about how to deal with them, and to be mindful when changes to the business might pose difficulties. As always, these aren't rigid guidelines to follow, but rather food for thought that can help you lead more intentionally.

Empowerment

Most managers think they empower their employees and most employees feel that they are not empowered. In this chapter we start with the question "Is your organization empowered?" Our unique twist on empowerment is that you have not truly empowered people unless you can cite instances when they did something knowing fully well that you think it is the wrong thing to do. Fear of empowerment is the fear of the empowered, shouts another article. And, the cost of un-empowered employees is illustrated in the example cited in the namesake article in this chapter.

A common question I am asked by CEOs of family-owned companies is whether they should have open-book financials. They usually fear that the employees would see the amount of money the company makes. My experience has been that employees build up a story in their heads that paints either a rosy or a doomsday picture of the health of the company. You might as well tell them what reality looks like. You are more likely to empower them to do the right thing.

Accountability and empowerment go hand in hand. You can't have one without the other. We combine both in the final article describing the Entrepreneur in Residence program.

Fear of Empowerment is the Fear of the Empowered

May 2013

Most CEOs want to empower their employees. They recognize the value, as well as the cost, of un-empowered employees. (See *The Cost of Un-Empowered Employees* on page 116). What they often do not appreciate, and usually fear, is the cost of empowerment.

But first, let's define empowerment.

Most people would define empowerment as encouraging and enabling others to make decisions and take actions. Do the actions of the empowered have to be the same as the inclinations of the manager? I speak to more than a thousand CEOs each year, and I often ask them this question. I am sure you have heard their response yourself. Their common response is, "No, [the subordinates] must be allowed to make mistakes and learn from them."

Have you ever stopped to think about the arrogance behind that statement? The CEO assumes that if the subordinate's course of action is not the same as the CEO's, then the subordinate's approach must be wrong. And in this case, the subordinate should be allowed to pursue that path to discover and learn why it is the wrong approach. That's where the disconnect lies between the CEO's claim of wanting to empower their people and their willingness to actually do so.

To truly empower people, you must fully accept the idea that difficult decisions can be made in a number of ways and you won't know which one is right until the future unfolds.

(See *Consensus: a Road to Mediocrity* on page 156).

Neither the CEO nor the subordinate can prove today that their approach is better. So the CEO who wants to empower their employees must accept that the subordinate's approach could very well be better than their own. Otherwise, the employees will sense that the CEO wants everything done their way and will not feel empowered.

Here's a good test to see if your organization is empowered:

Can your employees cite examples from the recent past, where an employee chose to pursue a certain path, fully knowing that it went against their manager's intuition? This is a tough test to pass but one worth taking nonetheless.

So why do we fear empowerment?

Because we fear what the empowered might do! You can easily understand that, occasionally, the empowered employee's approach might actually be better than your own, but when you're in the moment, it's difficult to accept. So you encourage your employees to follow your approach, and completely destroy your intent to empower them. To truly empower your people, you must have the courage to be in that moment and support your employee's decision. And you must allow for the success of that decision, even when it goes against your intuition – not because they need to learn from their mistake, but because they might do it in a better way than you thought possible. The fear of empowerment is the fear of the empowered.

I chose the title of this article, in part, because it can be read in two ways.

An alternative reading suggests that the fear of empowerment is instilled in the empowered.

A truly empowering CEO allows his or her employees to make decisions and take actions. And employees begin to understand and appreciate the responsibility that is being placed on them. Now they are not simply executing the decision of their superior, but rather executing their own decisions. Success and failure will now directly reflect on them, and that is scary!

The fear of empowerment is the fear of the empowered. Superiors fear empowered employees and the decisions they might make, and employees fear empowerment when they find themselves in the spotlight. That said, an empowered organization can do things that no CEO could ever do. Fear not, and empower them!

The Cost of Un-Empowered Employees

October 2010

This month's topic is less provocative but addresses a common problem: the cost of un-empowered employees. At our recent L³ leadership workshop in Vail, CO, a group of eight executives, almost all CEOs, went to an upscale restaurant in Vail that was run by a celebrity chef. With everyone settling in and some expensive bottles of wine ordered, we realized that the restaurant only offered a fixed menu with no à la carte options. Noting that the group had a commitment to go to a dessert event later that evening, we expressed our regrets to the waiter that we wouldn't be able to indulge in their dessert menu. At this point, everyone was in a good mood – wine was flowing and the group was clearly going to mean good business for a restaurant that was otherwise empty during the off-season.

At this point, one of the guests wondered if we could have another round of appetizers instead of dessert.

The waiter, not empowered to make that decision, went to check with the chef but told us that it likely wouldn't be an issue. Some time elapsed, and the CEOs began to discuss concepts of decision-making and empowerment that we'd been tackling in our workshop earlier that afternoon. Some predicted that a small additional charge would apply, which none of us would have minded.

But the waiter eventually returned to tell us the chef wouldn't deviate from the carefully designed menu she offered. This amazed the executives, and each began to wonder aloud if the customers and staff at their own companies might face similar situations. All through this conversation, the wait staff, being close to the situation at hand, realized the chef's decision – made from the kitchen – might leave eight unhappy diners. Out came the manager, only to tell us that if he'd known of the situation earlier, he might have been able to do something about it. But, unfortunately, the chef called the shots and he had to go along with her decision.

Un-empowered employees and a dis-empowered manager watched as eight dissatisfied voices left the restaurant.

We all wondered how the restaurant could have handled the situation better. Clearly, decision-making had been taken away from those that were closest to the issue. Even if the chef felt that she was making a sound decision, she should have recognized the gravity of the situation from the wait staff or personally approached our group to work out some kind of solution. Instead, the chef was more interested in her culinary creations than her customers' dining experience.

We found a perfect contrast the very next week when, at another event, six of us went to a similarly priced upscale restaurant called Cyrus in the Napa Valley. One person from my group made a similar request, and the wait staff's response inspired me to write this article. The waiter said, "Madam, I am confident the chef will find a way to accommodate your needs and make your dining experience exquisite." What a difference empowered employees can make!

Is Your Organization Empowered?
How Can You Tell?

August 2007

Most corporate leaders would like to think that the people in their organizations are empowered. The virtues of empowerment are acknowledged, respected and coveted. But what is empowerment? How can you tell if your organization is empowered? I propose a provocative definition of empowerment and suggest a way to tell if your organization is accordingly empowered.

I offer a workshop on speed and agility to corporate executives. An important component in achieving speed and agility is an empowered organization. So what is empowerment? Most intuitive – and formal – definitions of empowerment suggest that it is to enable or permit an individual, or a group of individuals, to make decisions and take action. Most corporate leaders want their organization to be empowered, in the belief that more can be achieved, with greater speed, by doing so. But in my opinion, few corporate leaders have fully fathomed its implications.

The leader must ponder a critical question. Assuming that the goals and objectives remain consistent with those of the leader, is the leader willing to let the members of the organization make decisions and take action that might be counter to the leader's intuition and inclination? If every decision and every action taken by the organization is required to be in alignment with the wishes of the leader, then the organization is not empowered. The only thing the leader has delegated is the "doing," not the "thinking."

A common misconception is that there is a "best" approach to business issues, situations or decisions, and that logic and reason, together with wisdom and experience, will reveal and convince others of the superiority of the "best" approach. An even further misconception is that the leader always knows best. In reality, the uncertainties of the future course of events make it impossible to discern the "best" approach and multiple viable options remain defensible. Further, the leader, based on extensive knowledge, wisdom and experience, might be more often right than wrong, but is, by no means, always right.

In a truly empowered organization, there will be many instances where individuals follow a path different from the leader's voiced preference, in the belief that such path is more effective in achieving the organization's goals. Such independence of thought and the resulting actions are what empower the organization. Furthermore, the leader's willingness to express an opinion but accept and respect the eventual choice made by the action-taker within the organization cultivates an environment of empowerment.

Based on this belief, I propose this test of empowerment: can people in the organization readily name a few instances in the recent past where somebody has chosen to follow a path that is known to be counter to the intuition of the leader? How readily can they recall such instances? How many can they recall? How did the leader react? I believe these questions are a telling test of empowerment.

Managerial Discretion: Its Privileges and Obligations

May 2014

Credit for this month's topic goes to Steve Cobb, chairman of Henny Penny, who shared this idea with us during a workshop I did recently with his executives.

Imagine this scenario: An hourly employee stuffing sausages at a sausage factory is expected to put in 40 hours a week and get paid for 40 hours of work. Occasionally, if the supervisor wants him to work extra hours to meet a deadline of sausage shipments, the hourly employee might agree to do so and be paid overtime. When the hourly employee takes time off or goes on a vacation, he expects somebody else to stuff sausages while he's gone, and he doesn't expect to find a backlog of unstuffed sausages at his workstation. In contrast, most – if not all – of you who read this article simply put in the hours needed to get the job done, which often requires more than 40 hours a week.

You have managerial discretion to prioritize and schedule your work based on the needs of the business and the needs of your personal life.

There are privileges and obligations that come with that discretion, and drawing attention to those privileges and obligations – to employees and management who are exempt – can be very valuable.

I once sent an email to a group of employees in the office, expressing my frustration at a behavior that I had observed.

These employees had total freedom in their work hours. They could come and leave at any time. They could take time off whenever needed. They had unlimited vacation time. Each of them had individual responsibilities, much of which was self-imposed and self-managed. All they had to do was to make sure that their work was done and done right. Yet I observed that they all left at the same time, around 5 p.m. each day.

This bothered me. Did they all happen to finish their work at the same time? Did it just coincide with a 5 p.m. quitting time? Or were some of them tired at 4 p.m. but didn't feel comfortable calling it quits for the day? Likewise, did some of them have pressing work beyond 5 p.m. but didn't feel obligated to stay late and get it done? Did the en masse departure at 5 p.m. mean they didn't fully comprehend the privileges and obligations of my managerial discretion?

So what are those privileges and obligations?

In contrast to a sausage stuffer who is expected to stand in a production line and stuff sausages, management has considerable discretion on the hours they keep, the quality of their work product and the scheduling of that work. They decide when the amount of research they have done or data they have collected is adequate to make the decision. They decide when the report is good enough to be shipped out. They decide what needs to be done now and what can wait or even be ignored. If they need to attend to their sick child or leave early for their child's baseball game, they do so and manage the impact. If they choose to work from home one day to get that project completed, they do so.

But with all that privilege comes obligation.

You are expected to err on the side of higher quality when deciding what is good enough. You are expected to work late, take work home in the evenings or work on weekends to ensure that critical projects are completed on time. You are expected to take on that extra workload when the unexpected happens, even though you already have a full workload. You define your hours not by the clock but by the work that needs to get done – it's always more than what the clock says.

While the privilege gives you a lot of freedom, the obligations impose a workload that adds up to more than 100 percent of your time.

And the higher you rise in management, the more privileges and obligations you take with you, resulting in greater disparity from 100 percent. I've tried to provide a rough idea of that disparity in the picture on the next page. Is it fair to expect management to regularly work much more than 100 percent of a regular workweek?

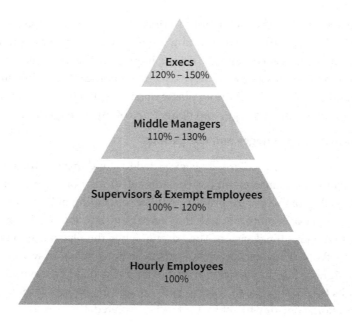

Execs
120% – 150%

Middle Managers
110% – 130%

Supervisors & Exempt Employees
100% – 120%

Hourly Employees
100%

Or is this a recipe for burnout?

Should this expectation be implicit, or should leadership explicitly discuss it with management? Would an explicit conversation lead to problems or resentment? If executive leadership doesn't work well beyond the regular workweek, can they expect lower level management to do so? In a private company with an operating owner, can the owner expect this behavior without walking the walk themselves?

I believe that management needs to fully understand this concept by cherishing the privileges and rising to the obligations. Top leadership raising awareness of these privileges and obligations will cause management to become intentional. In my experience, when top leadership brings attention to their privileges and obligations, it inspires management to become more intentional too.

A New Year Resolution: To Err

January 2008

My Speed and Agility workshop focuses on helping leaders create a more agile corporate culture by forming a specific decision-making process. And it starts with a simple question:

What are three important decisions made in the recent past that, in retrospect, you wish you had made sooner?

Not only do participants complete this exercise quickly, they often write down more than three. But when I ask them about decisions they wish they had deliberated longer, there is usually dead silence in the room. It's rare for even one person to offer an example. Why is that? It's human nature to endure the pain of the present while fearing the risk of change. Our upbringing, our schooling and our experiences have emphasized the value of being right more than the value of being fast.

Statistical quality control theory asserts that, in order to ensure the innocent aren't wrongly found guilty, one must either be willing to acquit the guilty on a regular basis or accept an arduous judicial process. But business decisions rarely have the gravity of decisions made in a court of law. There are two kinds of errors: finding the innocent guilty and acquitting the guilty. An organization can become more speedy and agile if management is more conscious of the costs associated with those kinds of errors. Instead, we usually let our instincts decide, favoring being right over being fast. But keep in mind, the "arduous judicial process" to resolve the issue also costs time.

My provocative New Year resolution is to make decisions fast and to have at least one example, by the end of the year, of pulling the trigger too quickly.

Should You Share Your Financials with Your Employees?

November 2011

Most would agree that it's good to educate employees on how the business runs – how much money comes in and where it comes from, how much money goes out and where it's spent, and what's left behind and how it's used to reinvest in the business.

Employees feel more invested when they understand the financials of the business.

They grow personally and professionally by understanding how the business makes money. They become more sensitive to the costs in the company. Even if they're not a shareholder, they develop a sense of ownership. So why don't more companies share their financials with employees?

Private companies worry whether it will expose their financials to the community, to their customers and even to the press, and whether their employees will be offended by the wealth being amassed by the owners. The smaller the company and tighter the ownership, the more this becomes a concern. But wait a minute! Do you really believe that your employees don't have a feel for the revenues of your company?

Employees in most companies, particularly small companies, tend to have a good idea of the company's revenues.

In contrast, employees of most companies "think" they have a feel for the expenses of the company. So in their heads they have a clear idea of the profits of the company and the amount of money the boss takes home.

Unfortunately, their estimate of the expenses is naïve and usually grossly understated. They underestimate the cost of the office or factory infrastructure; they are ignorant of employer expenses, such as a business license, business insurance and the employer's contribution to employees' tax obligations; they overlook a variety of costs such as utilities, janitorial services, equipment repair, maintenance, etc. So, it's understandable why they have an overstated estimate of how much the boss takes home. Without accurate information, employees fill in the blanks.

Educating your employees on the financial realities of your company creates a sense of empowerment and ownership.

And when you disclose that information, they're usually surprised by how much you spend on categories with which they're familiar and on which they have a direct impact. Your honesty encourages them to accept some responsibility in managing the expenses. As a result, they grow both personally and professionally.

Every employee in your company should have a good feel for the basic flow of your income statement – the sources and amount of revenue, and the classes and amount of expenses. In addition, your managers should also have a feel for the structure of your balance sheet – how much of your assets are tied up, where it is tied up and what return on those assets the company expects to get. Finally, your top executives should understand the nature of your cash flow and your capital structure – the periodic fluctuations in your working capital, your sources for cash (when needed) and an understanding of the leverage deployed in financing your business. By educating your employees in these areas, you're not just enabling them to do their jobs better, you grow them as employees – a stewardship responsibility you accepted when you hired them.

Accountability and Co-Accountability

February 2008

Your colleague commits to send you an email with some important information you need by end of day Tuesday. It's now end of day Tuesday, and you haven't received it. What do you do? Do you give them the benefit of the doubt and wait until Wednesday morning? Or do you give your colleague a few extra days as a grace period? Or do you contact the tardy colleague at 5 p.m. on Tuesday?

What is your obligation?

The inspiration for this *Food for Thought* came when a conscientious bystander in Germany took it upon herself to reprimand a jaywalker. It occurred to me that when people hold others accountable, those others hold themselves accountable.

Motivated by this observation, I experimented with a concept at one of our clients' companies.

The client had a corporate practice whereby latecomers to meetings dropped a dollar in a jar, earmarked for a charitable foundation. But when I asked how often the latecomers actually followed through, the client sheepishly admitted that people seldom paid. So I implemented a revised rule obligating the meeting participants to hold the tardy accountable. To underscore this obligation of **"co-accountability,"** the guilty latecomer had to call on all other meeting attendees to each drop a dollar in the jar if they failed to hold the latecomer accountable within a minute of their arrival. Lo and behold, latecomers quickly dropped a dollar in the jar before anybody could ask them to pony up.

The moral of these stories is that people will demonstrate a higher level of accountability in organizations where everybody – even a bystander – undertakes an obligation to hold individuals accountable. I call this responsibility **co-accountability**. It's really quite simple. To enhance accountability within organizations, people in the organization must accept the obligation of co-accountability.

Entrepreneur in Residence

September 2007

It's a sad fact that as corporations grow and mature, it becomes increasingly difficult for them to foster and promote entrepreneurship. All of those strict processes and layers of bureaucracy, instituted to protect a corporation's assets, end up becoming a hindrance to its entrepreneurial spirit. A brilliant idea for a new product or an opportunity to enter a new market dies on the vines of cafeteria conversations. Management's commitment to old ways of thinking creates too much resistance for bold ideas to flourish. A few might venture out of the company to become a brave startup. But others – in my opinion, most – simply return to pulling the corporate carriage.

If you're a CEO who finds this all too familiar and wants to promote entrepreneurship within your corporation, here's my suggestion: appoint an entrepreneur in residence, or EIR.

This idea isn't new. A study of entrepreneurship conducted 20 years ago credited 3M corporation as the originator, but even earlier versions were already in use. I helped implement the idea in its current form in one company. The basic idea is to appoint a capable mid-level manager as an EIR – someone senior management has considerable confidence in – and empower that person to gather, evaluate and execute entrepreneurial ideas from across the company.

Here's how it works.

Senior management, maybe the CEO, finds someone deep within the company who has shown considerable promise and appears to have significant headroom but hasn't risen to a senior-level management yet. Let's call this individual Jeanine. Presumably, the CEO has the utmost confidence in Jeanine and other departments are eyeing her for a new position. The CEO appoints Jeanine as an EIR, a title she carries in addition to her current duties and responsibilities. Besides the obvious prestige that comes with being appointed by the CEO, the EIR receives, figuratively speaking, a check for one million dollars (or any other reasonable dollar amount) to use on any legitimate business venture that she deems prudent for the company to pursue.

However, there are some constraints on the use of these funds. First, all expenditures and their accounting must conform to the company's standard policies and procedures. Second, the figurative check must be cashed within one year, during which time the EIR can explore many potential business opportunities as a side activity while performing her usual duties. Third is the most stringent constraint: the EIR must step down from her current position in the company to cash the check and start the new venture.

The idea behind an EIR is to create a better environment for entrepreneurial ideas to grow by bypassing a company's traditional management hierarchy.

When done right, an EIR instills a renewed sense of optimism in a company's innovators by encouraging them to pitch their ideas to the EIR the same as they would to a venture capitalist. An EIR can empower an organization that otherwise might complain of management being set in its ways by offering the employees an alternative non-management avenue of appeal. She creates excitement and buzz within the company, reinforcing the idea that individuals can make things happen. The intent is for the EIR to find inspiration from other innovators in the organization, or fully adopt their idea, and enlist them into the venture.

All that said, the EIR is unlikely to use the money callously. In fact, half the time the EIR won't even cash the check! For starters, the selection of the EIR by the CEO ensures that the individual has a good business mind and has a track record of accomplishments. Jeanine would not undertake a venture unless she felt confident that the venture could succeed. The EIR is likely to be even more critical of an innovator's idea than traditional management because she will seriously consider pursuing that idea with, in a sense, her own money. Lastly, to pull the trigger and cash the check, the EIR must sacrifice the security of her current position – not an easy task, even for the most confident individual.

The excitement of the EIR, the buzz within the company and the numerous cafeteria conversations that ensue are just the beginning. You could be the catalyst to an exciting new venture that pays off for your company.

And don't forget, until that check is cashed, the company has incurred no direct expense. And if a responsible EIR cashes the check, then there's a good chance the resulting business venture is a prudent investment.

Corporate Culture

With my dislikes of motherhood and apple pie, I have always been dismissive of posters that don't make a statement. When I see a poster in the lobby of a building that proclaims "honesty" as one of their values, I always wonder what alternatives they considered before they chose honesty as their preference.

In our own company, when "healthy relationships" was suggested as a value we wish to foster, I wanted to bring some edge to that statement and asked that healthy relationships be measured not by the number of hugs, but rather by the number of fights that end in hugs. In other words, if you want to implement a culture of healthy relationships, you should encourage an environment where disagreements and even arguments are acceptable as long as they always end in hugs.

Culture is usually viewed as soft subject matter. But I believe culture is solidified by institutionalizing concrete tools that provide a model for thought and action. In this chapter we offer some such models for thought and action.

Bet on Horses, Not on Races

April 2012

Last week, I launched a new program called Seven Secrets for Successful Leadership, and in this *Food for Thought,* I want to expand on one of those secrets: **Bet on horses, not on races.**

When you're looking to fill an open position in your company, you usually create a job description outlining responsibilities and duties and the skills and competencies you're looking for in a candidate. Then, you recruit people who seem promising, conduct interviews to see if they're a good fit for the job and the company and choose the person who seems best qualified.

Have you ever wondered why the job is fixed and why we try to find the right person to fill that job?

Instead, what if you found the best person available in the marketplace and explored how they could contribute to your company? Would they restructure their responsibilities based on the strengths they bring to the team? Would their presence create a shift in how workloads and responsibilities are distributed throughout the company? Would that be good for your company?

Undoubtedly, if you need a welding technician for your machine shop, the person needs to be good at welding.

But is that the definition of the job or is it just a basic requirement for someone who wants to be considered? If you define your basic requirements more narrowly, you can be broader in considering people. You might find people who bring the basic skill and a variety of other skills you didn't even know you could use. Instead of finding people to fill specific jobs, consider defining jobs to suit the good people you already have or good people who are available in the marketplace.

It was this idea that inspired me to conduct the exercise I describe in *Succession Planning Through Musical Chairs* **(See page 11).**

That exercise showed me that hiring managers were specific in their job descriptions and narrowly focused on the candidates they would consider.

But when they were forced to interview *any* interested candidate, often from significantly different backgrounds, the hiring managers were amazed by the various candidates' fresh ideas for approaching the job.

Lastly, in today's fast-paced world, the jobs that need doing are going to change over time. If you find a good person and structure the job around their unique abilities – and what's best for the company – you'll be more adept to change. Bet on horses, not on races.

Always Fast and Sometimes Wrong or Always Right and Sometimes Slow?

August 2010

This *Food for Thought* is motivated by a piece written by my friend and colleague Glenn Mangurian of FrontierWorks. In his monthly mailing called *Pushing the Edge,* he asks "Do you tend toward 'doing the right thing' or 'doing things right'?" With Glenn's piece as my inspiration, I want to pose a dilemma many corporations face in this age of fast moving markets where speed and agility are the crown jewels of corporate culture.

As a corporate leader, do you want to create a culture where people make decisions fast, even though some of those decisions might be wrong? Or would you rather have a culture where people deliberate to make the right decision, even though those decisions might cause the organization to move slowly?

The corporate world is littered with these kinds of dichotomies, and there is never a universally correct answer – neither a single correct answer for all situations nor a single correct answer for all people. But maybe we can better understand the issue by modeling it after the concepts of Type I and Type II errors in statistical process control (SPC).

In our situation, Type 1 error is the error of being wrong in a decision and Type II error is the error of being slow to make a decision.

SPC suggests that there is a heavy overhead cost to minimizing both Type I and Type II errors, beyond the costs of the errors themselves. More surprisingly, SPC indicates that balancing Type I and Type II errors also has a high overhead. So our natural tendency to balance the two types of errors has a high cost associated with it. On the other hand, SPC suggests that it's much more economical to operate with a bias, making one type of error more often than the other. To illustrate this point, consider taking it to the extreme. It's easy to operate in a way that ensures only one type of error will occur. For example, you can always wait until the right decision becomes obvious. You'll never be wrong, but you'll always be slow. Or you can make instantaneous, though questionable, decisions. You'll never be slow, but you're very likely to be wrong. More pragmatically, you need to understand your business and create a culture that's biased toward the more acceptable type of error.

So which error should you favor – the error of being wrong or the error of being slow?

In most corporate environments, when somebody makes a wrong decision, the error is pinned on the individual. But when somebody makes a late decision, the error is attributed to the culture. In that backdrop, which error do you think is the bias of most corporations? Most corporate executives would rather be slow than be wrong, but does that mean it's the right bias for all corporations? As your markets move faster, you might want to reassess the culture of speed and agility you're creating in your company. Ask yourself, which bias is the best bias for me?

Profanity in the Workplace and Its Impact on Your Brand and Culture

April 2014

Notwithstanding the stereotypes of Wall Street and the army, profanity use is usually not rampant in larger corporations where people tend to be more vigilant about following social norms, and daily interactions are more likely to include unfamiliar people. If used in larger companies, it is usually within a small group and in closed-door meetings. However, in smaller companies, where everybody knows each other and employees work together all day, the company's culture can unintentionally give unspoken permission for employees to freely use profanity in their routine interactions. Is that good or bad? What is the value and cost of such freedom? How does it impact your brand and your culture?

Should you create or prohibit a culture that accepts profanity? If so, how?

Advocates of profanity in the workplace are quick to qualify their position with restrictions: it should never be addressed at a specific individual or group; slurs directed at a specific gender, race, ethnicity, etc. are not allowed; it is never to be used in vain or in anger, but merely as colorful speech; it is never to be used in the presence of customers or clients; and if someone objects, those wishes must be respected.

The argument in favor of profanity use is that it provides a broader bandwidth of expression, allowing for people to communicate their passion with greater color. People can express their unfiltered position instead of beating around the bush. Swearing, when paired with humor, can relieve stress and release pressure from tense situations. Allowing people to speak in a way that resembles their social life makes for a more relaxed atmosphere, increasing camaraderie in the work place. You don't have to be on constant guard on what you might say and whom you might offend.

"If you accept that norm, what's the harm?" says the advocate.

Profanity can also be used as a weapon, a display of testosterone, a means of achieving personal dominance or a form of bullying. What level of profanity is acceptable, and when does somebody cross the line? Are graphic descriptions or pictures acceptable? Is each person left to decide what is acceptable based on their own comfort and that of their colleagues? Or does one have license to push the envelope until someone objects?

At one company I ran (a company that had started out as a startup but had grown to 250 employees) I discovered on my first visit that most of the offices proudly displayed calendars with photos of nude women. Interestingly enough, the offices without these calendars were occupied by women. Finding this practice very foreign to my own background in corporate America, I asked the women at the facility about the calendars. They told me they were uncomfortable with it but didn't feel like they could speak up. Clearly, if the situation gets to a point where one or more employees claim that it creates a hostile work environment, management would have to step in and put an end to it. Should management wait until someone objects? Is damage being done to the company even if no one objects?

If use of profanity is acceptable in the workplace, why is it restricted in interactions with clients?

Presumably, the premise is this: while you run around the house in your pajamas, you're probably going to wear a robe when you get the morning newspaper. But in the age of information, doesn't the outside world see you running around your house in your pajamas anyway? Do we really think that we can create one culture inside and a different brand outside? Shouldn't your brand and your culture be aligned?

What role does leadership have in either fostering or inhibiting the use of profanity in the workplace?

Isn't profanity a part of the culture that leadership creates – either unwittingly or intentionally? Should leadership take an intentional position, or should they let the organization find a level of *de facto* comfort? By now, you probably know what my answer will be. I believe it's important that leadership takes a clear position on the use of profanity in the workplace, communicates that to the organization and practices it at all levels. But my advice is not that you take my position, only that you take an *intentional* position.

A Startup on Your Premises Might Revive Your Startup Spirit

November 2012

Credit for this topic goes to Gary Baron, CEO of Voice Systems Engineering. Growth companies must work hard to maintain the speed, agility and entrepreneurship that brought them the growth they enjoy. But as a company grows, those very attributes are threatened. Gary Baron has an interesting solution.

When you need a specific talent for a task – a web designer to build your web pages, a lawyer to write a contract, an accountant to prepare your taxes, etc., your choice is to **hire or rent**. This is purely a financial decision. You decide that you do not have long-term needs for this talent or enough need to hire a full-time person, so you decide to rent the services on a fee-for-service basis. Typically, these are very specialized skills and the product they deliver (a web page designed, a contract prepared, tax papers filed) is usually, mostly objective. It's a simple, financial decision between hiring and renting. That's all.

But what if you opened up your office space to startups?

Assuming that you have an established office with some capacity for expansion, what if you offered suitable startup companies a home for a year? You might offer the startup free office space, including the usual office services such as a telephone, internet, printer/copy/fax machines, etc., for perhaps a year. During that year the (presumably few) employees of the startup hang out at your offices, interact with your people, bounce their ideas off your people during lunch conversations and the like. Maybe they pick up on some prudent processes and procedures from your company that a startup might not know how to do. Better yet, maybe they question some of your processes and procedures and force your employees to examine them too. Overall, the interaction is likely to be productive for both parties.

What do you get in return?

At a minimum, you get the influence of the startup. Additionally, you might structure it so that at the end of the year, you have the right of first refusal for any investment into that company. On top of that advantage, you would have had an entire year to closely examine this company before making any investment decision. You might even be perfectly positioned to provide manufacturing services, logistical operations, procurement efficiencies or distribution channels that such startups might not have on their own.

Many metropolitan areas and university communities have established similar concepts to give startups the infrastructure they need.

Where this idea differs is that, here, an established company provides space to a startup to reap the benefits of its influence. Gary Baron has done something similar in establishing the Novotorium, focused on assisting wellness and healthy lifestyle businesses. He's been doing this for a year and has learned important lessons from the experience. Requiring the entrepreneurs to have some "skin in the game" early on helps you find the seriously committed and eliminates those who bounce from one free program to another. He also found that this program can make a big impact on the established company, which is why he advises you to reach an investment valuation and agreement before the impact is realized. Finally, he found it important to establish a focus for the kind of startups you attract. Of course, one has to be mindful of any competitive issues both between you and the startup and between multiple startups that you might host.

Just imagine the kind of energy and spirit you would enjoy if you had a series of startups year after year. You might find that it generates a new startup within your own company!

Performing Versus Engaged Employees

October 2013

Performance management has become an over-used buzzword in the corporate world. Most companies understand the value of setting clear performance goals for employees. They evaluate the performance of their employees against those performance goals and provide the employees with feedback on what they have done well and where they might need improvement. We already value high-performing employees but do we value highly engaged employees? What's the difference?

Performing employees give to get.

Their focus is on the getting; they value what they get from the company. They get a good salary. They get to work in the town where they have social ties. They get good working conditions. They get good working hours. They value all that they get. They understand that to get all of those things, they must give to the company. So they do. They give their best efforts toward the company's goal. They do a good job so that they can get all the things they like. They're also more likely to be lured by an employer whom they can get more from, rather than one to whom they can give more. Their focus is on the getting. Giving is just the means by which they get. They give to get.

In contrast, engaged employees get to give.

Their focus is on the giving. The engaged employee is proud that they help people: they save lives, they teach others, they invent new things, they work on challenging projects, they lead a team, they make a difference. Their pleasure is in the giving. Getting is incidental. Yes, they have to pay bills, so they like getting a decent pay to live. But they work because they like what they do. Giving is the reason. They are more likely to be lured by an employer where they can give more than one who can give them more. Their focus is on the giving. They get to give.

Would you rather have a performing employee or an engaged employee?

No doubt, you probably would like an engaged and performing employee. Likewise, you probably won't tolerate a disengaged and non-performing employee for very long. Those are the easy cases. How about the hard cases? Would you rather have a well-performing employee that is struggling to be engaged or a well-engaged employee that is struggling to perform? People tend to prefer an engaged employee struggling to perform. Why is that? An engaged employee who is not performing is usually lacking some necessary skills. A performing employee who isn't engaged usually lacks the necessary attitude. This brings to mind a favorite quip: If you have an employee who doesn't have the skillset needed to do the job, give them a year to learn the skillset; If you have an employee who doesn't have the attitude needed to do the job, give them the entire weekend.

Should we be evaluating our employees just on their performance or also on their engagement? How do you evaluate people on their engagement? Does engagement change over time just as performance does? How frequently should you give employees feedback on their engagement? These are all questions worth considering. Ask yourself, do you have performing employees or engaged employees?

Celebrate the Slogger, Not Just the Brilliant

October 2011

Recently, I received some news about an old college buddy of mine, named Suresh, whom I met back in the early '70s in India. He came from very modest means, modest even by Indian standards, which means he lived way below the poverty line by western standards. Growing up in an environment where simply enrolling in high school meant exceeding expectations, Suresh bagged a scholarship to one of India's prestigious engineering universities. I spent five years with him in college and he was part of my close circle of friends. While most of us skipped classes now and then, Suresh never would. While we procrastinated in studying for the exam the next morning, he was studying diligently. Of course he was smart – he was admitted to that university, after all – but he was not the brilliant student in class whom others would seek out for academic help. In a college that produced acclaimed engineers and entrepreneurs, his performance received little recognition. But there was something about Suresh that my friends and I always noticed: his hard work and perseverance.

He was what we called a **slogger**. Admittedly, we assumed he had to slog to make up for the brilliance of his classmates. Little did we know, that slogger would become Major Gen. Suresh Chandra Jain, a top-ranking officer who would earn his PhD for technological advancements in the Indian Army.

We tend to notice, recognize and reward the brilliant – people who are smart and whose flashes of brilliance come out in memorable thoughts and ideas.

Flashes of brilliance are recognizable events; they are "Eureka!" moments that demand attention. A brilliant idea or an astute observation is often noted and recognized on the spot. The event becomes memorable. Yet have you ever noticed that we tend to associate the word "smart" with an attribute of an individual rather than an assessment of performance? We are more likely to say, "She is a smart lady," than, "She made smart contributions at the meeting."

Hard work and perseverance, on the other hand, aren't recognized the same way.

Hard work might be recognized over time, but there is no event marking its conclusion; no one yells, "Eureka!" when hard work is realized. As such, hard work might be noticed, possibly recognized and occasionally rewarded as it occurs. But, more likely, it's recognized and rewarded after the fact. And hard work is usually an assessment of one's performance rather than an attribute. We tend to say, "She worked hard on that project," rather than "She is a hard worker." And on the occasions when we compliment somebody as a hard worker, it often seems like a consolation prize compared to the trophy of being smart.

And yet, an employee who perseveres and works hard is likely to exhibit that behavior consistently. In contrast, a smart employee might occasionally come up with a smart idea but not all the time.

Ask anybody whether they would prefer brilliant employees who occasionally work hard or hard workers who are occasionally brilliant.

Chances are, they'll favor brilliance over hard work.

I'm not saying intelligence and brilliance aren't valuable, but rather that we tend to disproportionately recognize smart people without fully appreciating hard workers who persevere. My friend Suresh is a hard worker. He could not have accomplished all that he has if he weren't smart, but his trump card has always been hard work. Celebrate the slogger, not just the brilliant.

The Price of a Collegial Atmosphere

December 2015

In the U.S., we do not discuss politics at work. And if somebody expresses an opinionated position, we simply smile, nod and move on to the next topic. Why? Because politics polarize people and we want to maintain a collegial atmosphere at work. I grew up in India and I've spent a fair amount of time in Europe and Asia. Political discussions are not considered to be as polarizing in those regions of the world; they are simply viewed as a healthy debate.

Does a collegial atmosphere require a lack of disagreement?

In a collegial atmosphere, can people disagree, express their opinions with passion and conviction, and end the conversation by simply agreeing to disagree? We tend to believe that discussions must end in agreement or some sort of resolution. And this tendency can result in inauthentic conclusions to discussions.

Diffuse speakers relax their convictions and specific speakers dig in their heels for an argument. (See the February 2014 *Food for Thought, Are You Specific or Diffuse?* on page 20.) Do all disagreements have to be resolved one way or the other? Can people maintain healthy relationships fully knowing they disagree on certain important matters?

Healthy relationships are not measured by the number of hugs, but rather by the number of fights that end in hugs.

It's ending your fights with hugs that is important, not having a lack of fights. Healthy relationships should foster healthy debates. In fact, a lack of debates might be an indicator that your relationship isn't healthy.

In creating an intentional corporate culture, you might strive to create a collegial atmosphere. The shadow side of this strength is fear of conflict, where people are reluctant to express their opinion because it isn't aligned with the opinion being expressed by others.

Fear of conflict leads to loud and obnoxious voices drowning out the quiet and thoughtful ones. It leads to the multitude of subordinate opinions deferring to the single opinion of the superior. It leads to the new and different ideas being overwhelmed by the status quo of tried and true practices. In a culture with a collegial atmosphere, it is important that you empower, encourage and enable people to face conflict and have healthy debates.

How do you teach people to have a healthy debate?

Here are three common causes for debates turning ugly and, from these, three ways you can make debates healthy.

The first cause is Aristotle's principle of the excluded middle – the belief that there is a right and wrong. Something is either good or bad, either true or false, and you are on my side or you are with the enemy. This polarization of thought causes debates to become personal. What is the solution? Try throwing in expressions like, "I believe…" The more you use the term "I believe," the easier it is for the other person to receive your opinion. So do you turn everything into a belief?

That naturally leads us to the next reason debates turn ugly – facts versus interpretations.

In a wonderful book called *The Communications Catalyst,* my good friends and colleagues Mickey Connolly and Richard Rianoshek explain how people commingle facts and interpretations. By separating facts (that can be observed and measured) from interpretations (that are your way of looking at the facts and drawing conclusions from them), they argue that you can have more "accurate" and "authentic" conversations. Instead, people pursue "sincere" conversations where, by commingling facts and interpretations, they pursue "their truth," having convinced themselves that it is the truth. So separate facts and interpretations and preface your statements with those labels.

Finally, people ignore the old adage, "Seek first to understand, then to be understood." In my experience, the most important aspect of a healthy debate is the ability to understand and advocate the other person's point of view. (See the January 2013 *Food for Thought, Coaching through Advocacy* on page 7.) Showing that you can argue the other point of view demonstrates mutual respect for both parties. It also concedes the existence of multiple points of view and shows appreciation for the strengths of the opposing argument. Most importantly, it expresses recognition that opposing sides are not good or bad, right or wrong, based on the position they hold, and it leads to hugs at the end of fights.

Is Loyalty Good for Business?

July 2012

Would you like your employees to be loyal to you? Are you loyal to your employees? Is loyalty a good thing? Should we foster loyalty in our business, particularly between the employers and employee? What is loyalty anyway?

Be forewarned: my treatment of this subject has been known to raise eyebrows.

To understand loyalty, we should distinguish **loyal behavior** from plain, old, everyday **rational behavior**. What would be an example of a loyal behavior by an employee (toward an employer) that would be distinct from a rational employee operating in their best interest? Similarly, what would be an example of a loyal behavior by an employer (toward an employee) that would be distinct from a rational employer acting in the best interest of the company?

Let's look at an example. An employer might decide to hold on to their employees with make-do work during otherwise slow periods of business – not because it's easier to hold on to those employees for when business picks up, but rather because they feel an obligation to them. Likewise, an employee might forgo personal time or financial payouts to help out the employer during some difficult periods. In both cases, the implicit assumption is that the person's loyal behavior will pay off for them in the future.

With that in mind, here's my definition of loyalty: Loyalty is the practice of maintaining unrecorded items on the balance sheet of personal relationships.

By that definition, when an employee cancels their weekend plans to pitch in and meet a last-minute deadline at the plant, the plant manager profusely thanks the employee at the end of that weekend. In effect, the plant manager says to the employee, "I owe you one." Did the plant manager record a liability on their balance sheet, writing, "I owe this employee one?" No, it was an unrecorded off-balance-sheet liability that the company now holds. Likewise, the employee feels reasonably reassured that the company will note their extraordinary contribution and do something in return for the employee on a future date. The employee now holds an unrecorded off-balance-sheet asset.

The fundamental principle of loyalty is that these unrecorded off-balance-sheet assets and liabilities will eventually reconcile.

It is understood that, at a future date, there will occur another event with an offsetting asset/liability the other way. Even though these offsetting events don't cancel each other out dollar for dollar, one for one, over time both parties will eventually net something close to zero.

That is the principle of loyalty.

Loyalty is a great tool for small companies, for startups or for family companies.

Because it allows for cash flow without the use of cash. Loyalty allows the employer to conduct activities that might have otherwise consumed cash by having employees do extraordinary things for them by issuing unwritten IOUs. Likewise, the employee gets peace of mind and a sense of security knowing that they have been loyal to the employer. That is why small companies, startups and family companies often have a loyalty-based culture.

So when does loyalty break down?

When new people join the company and it grows, it no longer carries the same company history. Now devoid of history, actions taken by the company that might have been reasonable and sensible in the context of past events could now seem irrational or appear to be favoritism. When the company grows and history is lost, loyalty is likely to be misinterpreted. In other words, loyalty doesn't scale with size.

Worse, loyalty doesn't weather time well either!

With time, the unrecorded assets and liabilities begin to take on a life of their own. Both the asset holder and the liability holder constantly re-evaluate their holding in their favor! Pretty soon, what started out as a balanced sheet of IOUs fails to stay balanced, and there's no clear way to get back to zero. Loyalty does not scale with size or with time. As a company grows, it's forced to move on to something beyond loyalty. Loyalty is fantastic while it lasts, but don't get too attached to it if you want to grow. One day you will have to settle up and move on.

Engaging your Entitled Millennial Employee

November 2014

In this article, I'd like to focus on an inevitable truth you're probably all grappling with.

If you don't have any Millennial employees today, you will soon.

After all, they are the workforce of tomorrow. Born between the early 1980s and the early 2000s, Millennials will serve as the bulk of the workforce in 20 years. What makes Millennials different from the rest of us? Hasn't every generation been criticized by the previous when entering the workforce? Weren't the baby boomers called hippies and the Gen Xers labeled slackers?

So isn't it wrong of me to call Millennials entitled? Probably. But let's chalk it up to carrying on an age-old tradition. Now, let's determine how Millennials are unique as a generation. I should first say many of the observations I make are based on current American society and might not apply to the cultures of foreign readers – although I suspect there are many similarities.

Millennials are accused of wanting everything given to them, and some people believe that everything has been.

A common perception is that Millennials feel entitled to a college degree in a discipline with little employment opportunity; they hang out in their parents' basement; they work as baristas at the local Starbucks and update their Facebook and Instagram accounts on their iPhones, which are part of the family plan just like their healthcare. As Catherine Rampell of *The Washington Post* writes, "To some, this arrested development is evidence of a prolonged adolescence and a rejection of self-sufficiency, perhaps encouraged by indulgent helicopter parenting."

The Great and Silent generations, which have retired from the workforce, found a loyal employer and gave them their working life. For the "one-company" professional, being engaged in their job was essential. The baby boomers and the Gen Xers realized that there was no guaranteed employment. Instead, they had to guarantee their own employability. So they devoted their working life to a career, albeit with different employers. Like the "one-company" professional, the "one-career" professional knew that being engaged and getting the most out of their job was in their best interest. The Millennials, on the other hand, seem to center their choices upon a particular lifestyle. They choose a lifestyle and construct the necessary underpinnings of work, family, relationships, etc. to support that lifestyle. Will that lifestyle be the constant in their life? Only time will tell. But meanwhile they are convinced their lifestyle is what's most important. Engagement in the job? Only to the extent that it supports their lifestyle!

So how do you engage your Millennial? Understand their lifestyle!

In the "one-company" view of the world, it was possible for employers to invoke JFK's language, rallying their employees around the message, **"Ask not what your company can do for you, but ask what you can do for your company."**

That rallying cry still worked in 1980 when Lee Iacocca used a variation of it at Chrysler after returning from Washington with a loan to save the company. It even worked as recently as 1995 when IBM's Lou Gerstner made a similar appeal in the name of saving "the greatest computer company of the world." Can you even imagine making that appeal today? Imagine if you did. How would your employees respond? Now compare that response to the generation they belong to. Do you see a pattern?

I've discussed the concept of loyalty in a company before in the July 2012 article, *Is Loyalty Good for Business?* on page 144.

A culture of loyalty encourages going over and above the call of duty when the company needs you.

All cultural benefits have a weakness I like to call the shadow side. In the case of loyalty, the shadow side can be entitlement. The employee argues that if they are expected to do something for the company when the company needs it, the employee should expect the company to be there when the situation is reversed. This sense of entitlement permeates loyalty-based cultures. When Millennials enter into such an environment, they are more likely to grasp one side of the equation and not the other.

Why don't Millennials give as much?

Are they just takers? Not really. In fact, some argue Millennials are more concerned with worthy causes than previous generations. They were raised in a generation where doing good – good for people, good for the environment, good for the disadvantaged, good for different races, etc. – was in vogue. Their apathy toward corporate America stems from a different source.

Millennials entered the workforce just as the market crashed in 2008.

The recovery never trickled down to them, and they don't believe it ever will. Millennials operate under a different value system. Their **utilitarian economics**, if I can call it that, is very different from previous generations'. Whereas previous generations readily exchanged their time for money, Millennials find a very different balance in that equation. Previous generations had a low discount factor for the value of their time, whereas Millennials put less trust in long-term investments and apply a high discount factor. Whereas the previous generations respected their predecessors for their knowledge and experience, even when telling them to modernize, Millennials believe the non-digital generations are dinosaurs who can teach them little. Finally, the Millennials saw how their parents worked hard only to get nowhere, and believe the time they invested just wasn't worth it. The Millennials aren't going to do that.

So how do you engage them?

We have to understand their lifestyle. In keeping with one of my tools, *Coaching Through Advocacy* (See page 7), we have to be able to advocate their point of view. The more we understand Millennials and their unique perspectives, the healthier our businesses will be in the future. And just like the future, the Millennials are coming. And they're coming fast.

Succession Planning in a Family-Owned Business

August 2015

Over the years, I have helped many owners of family-owned businesses plan for, think through and execute the transition of their businesses to the next generation – be it the next generation of the family, the next generation of management or the next generation of ownership.

In all cases, I noted one common weakness: they started the planning when they already had a transition date in mind.

Why is that a problem? Because they were looking for a plan to execute rather than pondering the philosophy that should drive the plan. In other words, if you haven't started thinking about this, it may already be too late. Let's elaborate.

During any management transition in a company, chances are that, in the short term, the income statement is preserved. But the balance sheet can be destroyed, unwittingly and unnoticeably.

I don't mean the financial assets or even the tangible assets of the balance sheet, but rather the intangible assets that were never recorded on the balance sheet. After a management transition, people will still continue to bring in the orders, produce the products, deliver the services and keep things running. But that only ensures that the income statement for the next few periods is protected. Meanwhile, the brand of the company, its corporate culture, its atmosphere, company morale and level of employee engagement are all affected. If the company was successful before the transition, then after the transition these intangible balance sheet assets can (at best) be protected or (at worst) be destroyed. This is even more important when a family-owned business transitions, because the success of the transition and the legacy of the family are closely linked. Planning for this success should begin long before planning for a transition, and it should begin with the philosophical intent.

There is a difference between the philosophy behind a plan and elements of the plan.

Let's illustrate with three examples. One client who thought through his succession wanted to ensure that the culture of the company stayed intact. At the same time, the owner was looking for a graceful exit strategy to liquidate his equity. How can you sell the company to somebody else and yet require that the culture stay intact? He found a solution!

Another client wanted to transfer the company from one generation of the family to the next. Though they wanted to transfer the equity and management, they wanted the "patriarch" to stay in a consulting role. "Is that possible?" they asked. This company found a solution, with partial success.

Yet a third client wanted to create an exit strategy for the owners while preserving the operational culture as a strategic selling point. The company has since been sold, and the owners tell me the parent company has now adopted some of the cultural practices. In all three cases, the owners had a clear philosophical intent, which drove the creation of the plan.

So what is the secret? Actually, there are three secrets.

Start planning long before you think you need to start. Think philosophy before thinking about a plan of action. Stop commingling management transition with ownership transition.

I offer a seven-step process, assuming you're starting this process long before you have to execute it.

Step 1: Understand what matters to you.

If your answer is "liquidating your equity," or "taking care of the people," etc., you aren't digging deep enough. So how do you dig deep? Try this admittedly morbid exercise. Imagine what you will think about during the last 24 hours of your life. How does it feel playing that out in your head? For most of us, it's too uncomfortable. Here's an alternative exercise called Inspired Imperatives, a collection of fundamental beliefs you hold dear and would be proud to have lived by. I teach this technique in my Beyond L³ program, the graduate-level course offered after my leadership program. Whichever exercise you choose, the outcome should create a simple list of what matters to you. This will serve as the foundational philosophy for the creation of your succession plan.

Step 2: Build bench strength.

Most CEOs of successful family-owned businesses are natural leaders who have never given thought to their style of leadership. One consequence of that lack of intentionality is that those CEOs have not caused others to become intentional leaders. They typically do not have bench strength. The most common limiting agent for a growing family-owned company isn't market opportunity or investment capacity; it's the limited leadership talent below the CEO. Senior leadership frequently focuses so exclusively on the growth of the company, that it often neglects growing its internal leadership, the fuel the company needs for continued growth. So focus on developing intentional leadership throughout your organization.

Step 3: Articulate the company story.

It's important for companies to have an organizational narrative. Most family-owned companies have a story – it usually starts out with how the company was founded and how it transformed over generations. Initially, the company and the family were commingled. The purpose of the company was drawn from the CEO's purpose, and in most successful family-owned companies, the CEO is a benevolent patriarch – I use the term patriarch in lieu of a gender-neutral noun. Sufficed to say, the company adopts the CEO's vision with enthusiasm. That's the company story.

But an organizational narrative should cover a broader range of topics. The company's story, including its origin and the founding family, and the source of the company's core purpose need to be woven into the organizational narrative. It should also include the company's vision of the future, the mission it has adopted to bring that vision to reality, and the core values that govern the behavior in the company. The CEO carries it in their head today. It needs to have life in the future.

Step 4: Institutionalize the company culture.

Most successful family-owned companies have an implicit culture, usually driven by the benevolent patriarch who is viewed as the culture's caretaker. The elements of the culture are implicit understandings, which over time have created implicit cultural pillars. For example, respect for leadership might be a cultural pillar that has always existed, usually because of the respect for the patriarch. A collegial atmosphere might be another such cultural pillar. But these cultural pillars usually have a weakness that I call the shadow side. The shadow side of respect for authority might be self-imposed lack of empowerment, where middle management doesn't do anything until checking with senior leadership first. A collegial atmosphere's shadow side is a feeling among staff that it's not considered acceptable to disagree with someone in a meeting. During the management transition in a successful family-owned company, the pillars can crack, leaving the shadow side weaknesses exposed. Family-owned companies are also known for creating a loyalty-based culture. But are they intentionally loyalty-based or intentionally deciding to remain that way? It's crucial for the patriarch to institutionalize an intentional culture that will outlast them, and in the process, ensure that the shadow side weaknesses are mitigated.

Step 5: Develop an equity transition plan.

Do not commingle the transfer of equity with the transfer of management. They are two separate items and should be considered separately. They might interweave, but they should do so intentionally. Is the equity going to be transferred within the family? If so, will it be transferred by gift, inheritance or purchase? Engaging a competent financial advisor to facilitate this conversation can make these awkward discussions more honest and direct. Is the equity going to be transferred to management? If so, what is the timeframe and who are the participants? Is the equity going to be sold to an outside investor? If so, has the family accepted the consequences? Has the family considered an ESOP arrangement? All of these questions should be answered with Step 1 in mind and with an independent professional advisor who can articulate the pros and cons, independent of the management transition plan.

Step 6: Develop a management transition plan.

Is management going to be transitioned to another family member or to an outside CEO? In either case, will the new successor be in residence, apprenticing for the job? If so, will the plan be put in place, communicated to all parties concerned (including the top leadership) and allowed to move down the grapevine before the transition occurs? Are there constraints placed on the new management? For example, the family might have a requirement that the plant in their small town not be disrupted. Or they may decide that a certain customer, product or employee is off-limits and that new management cannot discontinue their engagement unilaterally. Although these requirements can be purely emotional, they must be clearly communicated. The patriarch also needs to be clear with the new management as to the extent of involvement they intend to have. This plan should be in place before a successor is chosen.

Step 7: Execution.

Now you can begin to talk timeframe and execution. Clearly, there are execution elements in each of the previous steps. Put all of those execution elements in a PERT chart so that dependencies become clear and the critical path becomes evident. Use that chart to decide on a timeframe and to lay out the action steps that need to occur.

I have used elements of this plan with various clients. If you're facing this challenge firsthand, starting early and being intentional will be critical to a successful succession plan in your family-owned business.

Decision-Making

Decision-making is arguably the most common activity of management. Yet it is probably the biggest weakness of most organizations. In the article *Consensus: a Road to Mediocrity*, we argue that consensus has a time honored reverence of being a noble and egalitarian approach. Yet it seldom works. I believe people confuse consensus decision-making and consultative decision-making to be synonymous. No doubt consensus is a consultative form of decision-making. But it is not the only form.

There is a general desire in our society for everybody to agree. We find it incomplete to close a conversation with the understanding that there are different opinions and that no amount of further deliberation is going to truly convince one party of the other party's position. Yet that is the reality of life.

This is probably the topic in which I have made the biggest contribution in the leaders and organizations I have influenced. Although I have gone through this process multiple times, I am always reminded of how difficult it is to institute a good decision-making process.

Consensus: a Road to Mediocrity

July 2008

Consensus is honored as a noble, egalitarian approach to decision-making. But does it really yield a superior decision or just a more palatable one?

I believe that, in a corporate environment, consensus is usually achieved through one of four fallacious means, and the resulting decisions lead you down a dangerous path – the road to mediocrity.

The reasoning behind consensus-based decision-making is that constructive, collaborative conversations will render the best solution self-evident to all. But in today's corporate world, where speed and agility are critical, if the best option for a difficult decision has uniquely distinguished itself to be self-evident, then management must be guilty of procrastination.

With decisions having to be made sooner and quicker, consensus is often reached through one of these fallacious means, resulting in the dreaded mediocre decision:

- **Deference to authority:** Even a casual opinion of the boss can quickly lead to a consensus decision. You just overpaid for one person's opinion, and all you got was a mediocre decision.

- **Compromise:** Know the difference between a superior solution with input from all and a compromised solution that accommodates the interests of all. The former creates value; the latter leads to mediocrity.

- **Bartering:** Sometimes individuals suppress reservations and disagreements to gain favor in future decisions of greater importance. When this happens, value has shifted from corporate goals to individual agendas. Mediocrity is just around the corner.

- **Apathy:** When repeated meetings and conversations – regurgitating the same arguments over and over again – do not lead to a consensus, it is surprising how many people simply give up and consensus ensues. The loud and obnoxious argument, rather than the best argument, usually wins, but mediocrity is the real winner.

So is there a better form of decision-making that preserves the value of constructive, collaborative conversations but avoids the pitfalls of consensus? Yes, we call it the Authority style of decision-making.

Don't Confuse Indecision With No Decision

September 2012

Are you or your organization wanting to make a decision but unable to do so? Do you find that you have gathered all the data you can get and considered the options but can't decide which way to go? Would you call that indecision or lack of a decision? Let me offer a distinction. **Indecision** is an individual's inability to make a decision. **A lack of decision** is the organization's confusion as to how a decision is going to be made. Both are harmful to the organization.

Decisions that have a deadline force a conclusion.

Should we extend the lease or find new space? Should we make a tax-efficient investment for this tax year? Should we hold a holiday party? These questions have deadlines, and a decision is put off until the deadline. In contrast, decisions that have no deadlines often lead to indecision. Should we open a branch in that other town? Should we hire an additional marketing professional? Should I invest in developing my people or myself? In most of these situations you are convinced you should eventually do so but wonder if now is the right time.

Leaders sometimes spend so much time thinking through the issue that they end up incurring more costs for their time than the cost of any risk they might undertake in that decision.

Indecision is usually the result of a person's unwillingness to take risk. Usually, they have considered all the options but are unable to predict how the future will unfold. Decisions are actions taken today whose validity will only be realized when the future unfolds. In fact, if the best option for a difficult decision becomes self-evident, you might well be accused of procrastination!

The best way to deal with indecision is to have a self-imposed deadline. I recommend declaring it publicly.

But don't forget, you can make the decision to not make a decision until a future deadline. Again, such a deadline should be established and declared publicly. These techniques force you to minimize wasted time while bringing closure.

A lack of a decision is often a bigger organizational problem.

You often find people in the organization claiming, "No decision has been made on that issue." What it really means is that they have no clue as to who, how and when a decision is going to be made. Indecision, on the other hand, is usually a characteristic of questions without a deadline. A lack of decision can be found in questions with and without a deadline. A lack of decision is really the decision to let the status quo prevail. Lack of decisions maintain status quo and inhibit change in the organization, making them stagnant and slow to move.

Arguably, decision-making is the most common activity of management.

Organizations must have a clear decision-making process. The leader of the organization should establish the process and promote its deployment throughout the organization. While I have my opinions on the various decision-making processes (see *Consensus: a Road to Mediocrity* on page 156), any process is better than no process. Both indecision and lack of decision are harmful to the organization. Too much time is wasted discussing issues without a clear conclusion to show for it. And the leader is responsible in both cases: for their own indecision and the organization's lack of decisions.

Even Better than a Split Vote is a Mixed-Up Split

June 2013

This *Food for Thought* is motivated by a U.S. Supreme Court decision that came down in June of 2013. The decision revolves around whether routine collection of DNA samples – taken from people accused of a serious crime – is a violation of their right to privacy granted by the Fourth Amendment of the U.S. constitution. To all non-U.S. readers who might have no interest in this issue, hang in there! I am about to connect it to leadership and business in a way you will find interesting! The justices of the Supreme Court were split on this decision, which isn't that unusual since the court is often split on major decisions.

The unusual aspect about this decision was that the split was *not* along ideological lines – conservatives on one side, liberals on the other.

Rather, Justice Beyer, a liberal justice, sided with the conservatives, while Justice Scalia, a conservative justice, sided with the liberals. They both had good arguments for their positions, and the nature of that split inspired this article.

Decision-making in a commercial, for-profit business environment is a common theme for many of my *Food for Thought* articles.

I advocate decision-making through delegation of authority to one individual, as opposed to arriving at a decision by consensus, democracy or by command from the top. (See *Consensus: a Road to Mediocrity* on page 156.) In fact, I say that if the best solution to a difficult decision becomes self-evident to all, then the organization and its leader can be accused of procrastination. By that logic, I argue that when difficult decisions are made in a timely fashion, half your staff should disagree with that decision. This line of reasoning encourages division of opinions among a group of people working together. In other words, I really encourage split opinions.

However, in many organizations, the members align themselves into camps.

Eventually, split opinions divide the same group of people into each camp. In business, this kind of ideological stubbornness seriously reduces effectiveness. Pretty soon, a leader emerges from each camp and the two leaders duke it out. The value of X number of independent opinions is reduced to two unwavering group opinions. Furthermore, the more often this happens, the more groupthink begins to set in. As much as I argue that there should be a divided opinion on difficult decisions, I also argue that having the same division repeatedly is not healthy. So even better than split decisions are mixed-up splits.

What is healthy is a staff that can discuss decisions candidly and constructively, and accept that everybody will not be on the same side on major decisions. This staff will regularly form mixed groups in split decisions. They'll be more independent in their thinking and will more readily accept differences of opinions, since it's not one camp against the other.

A Holiday Tradition

The December 2007 article *The Spirit of the Holidays: Scrooge or Santa* sets the stage for this chapter. It started a tradition we continued for many years. In subsequent years, some of our clients adopted the tradition as well. Many of our clients would comment on this tradition as something they remembered of our articles, and they would talk about it with their colleagues.

The idea was to pay it forward. The holiday season is not about what you get, but rather what you give. After all, for every "get" is a "give."

In 2014 under our new company, Think Shift, we expanded the idea to a broader concept. Although you cannot participate in the tradition, I hope reading about it brings cheer in your life and a desire to give.

The Spirit of the Holidays: Scrooge or Santa?

December 2007

In the spirit of the holidays, I thought I would raise two seemingly unrelated questions about the appropriateness of corporations making charitable contributions and spending money on holiday greeting cards. Should corporations, both public and private, where management and ownership are separate and distinct, spend shareholders' money on charitable contributions to worthwhile causes? In the name of good corporate citizenry, should management make charitable contribution decisions based on their individual and personal favors and dispositions? For example, is it OK for the CEO to support their favorite cause, say the American Cancer Society – admittedly, a noble and reputable organization? How about the CEO supporting the local "Foundation for the Emancipation of Animals held in Captivity in Zoos," a cause that might be more controversial than a cause like fighting cancer?

The late Sir James Goldsmith – a controversial character in his own right – once said, "Don't confuse doing business with doing good." You do "business" to make money so that you can do "good." A for-profit corporation's purpose is to make money for its shareholders. Let the shareholders decide if and how to do "good" with that money.

Hence, I posit that a corporation's charitable contributions should be limited to those causes that further its business interests. Management makes a business decision on whether the charitable contribution is a worthwhile way to spend their marketing dollars to further the company's products and image. Accordingly, it might be appropriate for Pfizer to contribute to the American Cancer Society but more questionable for Nike to do so. Likewise, Nike might find it beneficial to contribute to the cause of disadvantaged inner-city kids as a way of promoting its image within a targeted constituency.

Charitable contributions by corporations should be purely a business decision for a business purpose.

Before I am characterized as Scrooge, let us move on to holiday greeting cards. What is the purpose of a corporation spending money on holiday greeting cards? Presumably, it is an opportunity to re-establish contacts with clients and business colleagues using the greeting card as a vehicle for that reminder. This probably makes good business sense. Many of us practice it.

At LogiStyle, we have always sent out greeting cards at this time of the year. Even at a small company like ours, we spend in excess of $1,000 on this practice. Just imagine how much large corporations must be spending. In fact, some companies decide to use the money instead for a charitable cause and simply communicate by email with their business colleagues that they have chosen to do so in lieu of sending holiday greeting cards. Have such companies achieved their business purpose of reconnecting with their business colleagues and reminding them of their association? At least a physical greeting card requires some handling and action. A passive email, on the other hand, significantly compromises the original intent, though the money has gone to a good cause. Hasn't the company just made a charitable contribution without meeting its business purpose?

In keeping with our brand, we offer a provocative way of combining the two intents: reconnecting with colleagues and supporting a good cause. The company sends an email to its business colleagues inviting the recipient to make a personal charitable contribution to his or her favorite charitable cause, upon which the company would make a matching contribution to that cause. This might cause the recipient to take notice of the email greeting card from the company and achieve the intended purpose of the greeting card. Imagine if all, most, many or even just a reasonable number of companies adopted that approach.

At LogiStyle, we decided to adopt this approach, with this article serving as our proxy for the greeting card. You are invited, as a recipient of this mailing, to make a charitable contribution to your favorite cause – subject to certain requirements – and we will match up to $100 of your contribution, limiting this offer to a total of $1,000 of matching contributions on a first-come, first-served basis. The charitable organization must be a non-profit organization under IRS Section 501(c)(3) and cannot be a religious organization. This offer cannot be applied to past contributions you have already made.

We will make a matching contribution to your chosen cause and inform you immediately that we are doing so. We will also publish the names of the people who responded and received matching contributions in our next month's *Food for Thought.*

Our hope is that with this provocative approach both our intended purposes will be served. You will be caused to pause and ponder, possibly take us up on it, maybe even bring the topic up at your holiday cocktail party. And we will together contribute to some worthy causes.

A Provocative Holiday Tradition

December 2008

As I am writing this over the Thanksgiving weekend, it is only fitting and proper that I thank the readers of *Food for Thought*, many of whom have commented on how these ideas make you think. Conversations with numerous executives that we meet every month serve as fodder for coming up with a new, provocative, and possibly controversial, idea each month and developing a logical argument in support of it. Nevertheless, this month we are recycling an idea from one year ago, in part because it is fitting for the upcoming holiday season and, in part, because we wish to make a tradition of it.

In December 2007, we examined the appropriateness of hired corporate management making charitable contributions to their favorite charities using their shareholders' money. In the same breath, we questioned whether corporations who send out holiday emails, indicating they have donated to charity in lieu of sending out holiday greeting cards, reap the "touch and contact" benefits intended by the traditional practice of greeting cards. With that backdrop, we offered a provocative proposal that we repeat this year.

Imagine if corporations adopted the following approach. The company sends an email to its business colleagues inviting each recipient to make a personal charitable contribution to his or her favorite charitable cause, upon which the company would make a matching contribution to that cause. This might motivate the recipient to take notice of the email greeting card from the company and achieve the intended purpose of the greeting card.

At LogiStyle, we have decided to adopt this approach, with *Food for Thought* serving as our proxy for the greeting card. You are invited as a recipient of this mailing to make a charitable contribution to your favorite cause – subject to the requirements below – and we will match up to $100 of your contribution, limiting this offer to a total of $1,000 of matching contributions on a first-come, first-served basis. The charitable organization must be a non-profit organization under IRS Section 501(c)(3) and cannot be a religious organization. (Our apologies to our non-US recipients.) You must send us an email by December 15 with the following information:

- The name of the charitable organization and its contact info.

- Your name and the amount of your intended contribution.

- A pledge that you will make the indicated contribution by the end of the calendar year. This offer cannot be applied to past contributions you have already made.

- A statement from you indicating that LogiStyle is permitted to publish your name, the amount and recipient of your contribution in next month's *Food for Thought* mailing.

We will make a matching contribution – limited to the constraints above – to your chosen cause and inform you immediately that we are doing so. We will also publish the names of the people that responded and received matching contributions in our next month's *Food for Thought* mailing.

Our hope is that, with this provocative approach, both our intended purposes will be served. You will be caused to pause and ponder, possibly take us up on it, maybe even bring the topic up at your holiday cocktail party. And we will together contribute to some worthy causes. Please do respond to this offer. In any case, have a Happy Holiday and a prosperous New Year.

Paying It Forward: A Glimmer of Hope for the New Year

January 2009

Last month, we continued our provocative holiday tradition of inviting you to donate to charity and offering to match your donations in lieu of spending on greeting cards. We want to start the new year off with some good news, recognizing that we could all use some good news in these tough economic times. First of all, our offer of matching donations was fully subscribed. We matched the donations of 11 individuals, totalling $1,000, made to nine different charities.

But more rewarding was that one recipient of these *Food for Thought* mailings, Glenn Mangurian, principal of FrontierWorks of Hingham, MA, chose to launch his own similar offer for the holidays to his network of clients and friends in lieu of spending on greeting cards. His offer, too, was fully subscribed, with 10 individuals donating to 10 charities. This is just what we had originally intended for this provocative thought. Imagine the viral effect possible.

But wait – there's more! One of Glenn's contacts, Arthur Bourque, CEO of Surveillance Specialties, Ltd. of Wilmington, MA, liked the idea so much that he offered to double up on Glenn's mailing and match the next 10 donors. Now that is the spirit of giving.

To begin this new and potentially difficult year we wanted to use our first *Food for Thought* mailing to tell you about how these ideas influence others, particularly in this heartwarming way. We hope you had a relaxing holiday and a great start to the New Year.

Making Nice Happen

December 2014

This article went out in the middle of the month for a joyous reason:

We, a collection of companies, made *Nice* happen.

In past years, starting with our December 2007 *Food for Thought*, we have used our holiday article to promote an innovative pay-it-forward approach. With our recent merger, we wondered what our new company, Think Shift, should do. We wanted to keep it innovative and provocative, in keeping with our *Food for Thought* articles, but we also wanted to promote the idea of giving.

Earlier this year, I invited you and your companies to join in a new idea. Many of you responded, and our company, Think Shift, was joined by three other companies, Décor Cabinets, GHY International and The Chopping Block, who were also interested in making *Nice* happen.

Each of the companies sent their employees out to one or more of the communities where they operate and asked the employees to do something *Nice* for somebody who needed it.

And they did.

Each company planned their activity, made *Nice* happen and sent us their footage. We compiled the footage and, each company plans to share it with their clients, customers and partners. All of us, in our own way, and in our own communities, made *Nice* happen.

The excitement of the holidays is in the air and 2014 is drawing to a close. All of us at Think Shift want to take this opportunity to wish you Happy Holidays and an exciting New Year. We appreciate our interactions with you and hope to enrich that for both of us in the coming year.

Miscellaneous

This chapter is exactly what the title suggests: everything that didn't naturally fall into one of the other categories. I have some of my favorites in this section. For example, although the popular wisdom suggests that a face-to-face conversation is far preferable to an email conversation, I argue in *The Power of Electronic Conversations* the value of the latter.

The article *Don't Discount; Give it Away for Free* is a landmark article because I have used it multiple times. It is my common tool to support my philosophy of not discounting our workshops and services.

Finally *A Spoonful of My Own Medicine* lays out the process I went through to merge LogiStyle and Think Shift.

Play Musical Chairs With Your CEO Group

August 2012

This *Food for Thought* article is most pertinent to presidents and CEOs of companies – especially those who are members of CEO groups like TEC, Vistage, YPO, EO, Gazelles and the like. If you fall into one of these categories, it is likely that you are part of a group that meets regularly. Your group is also likely facilitated by a chairperson and filled with other members who have become trusted advisors for you – you might be very open with them about your company and even yourself. Assuming all of those things, here is a thought for you to consider.

Imagine you're at one of your group meetings and your chair asks everybody to stand up, move over one seat and sit down. Then he or she suggests that you spend the next week running the company of the person who previously occupied that seat.

For a week, you abandon your responsibilities in your own company and go to work at your friend's company as its acting president/CEO. You run that firm and all its daily operations for a whole week. You talk to the executives and employees there, asking them questions that might appear basic and ill-informed in their eyes, questions about what they do and why they do it the way they do. You ask them if they thought of doing it a different way. You force them to explain to you the rationale behind their policies, practices, decisions, etc. I bet a week of questioning by an outsider CEO is going to create a lot of new thought in that company's staff.

Can you really do this? Is it safe and prudent to hand the keys to your company to another individual?

But is the individual really a stranger? After all, don't you lean on this individual as a trusted advisor in your CEO group? Imagine the value of those unbiased questions and the insight of a trusted outsider. Imagine its value in a context where the real boss is not present to defend or criticize. In contrast, imagine the value your own company's staff will get if the situation were reversed.

Even if you do not do this with the whole CEO group, it might be possible to do this by mutual swaps between two to four CEOs.

In fact, doing this periodically with different companies – say, once a year with different rotational assignments – will provide new and distinct value each time around.

What harm can happen?

Will the acting CEO make some senseless decision that sinks the company? Will the acting CEO become a rabble-rouser who leaves your executive team or employees disgruntled? Are you concerned that the acting CEO might make you look deficient? Will activities in your own company come to a grinding halt because you're gone for a week, leaving your company with an acting CEO? I believe there are ways to relieve the majority of these concerns. The biggest concern is probably the uncertainty it creates in your mind, but uncertainty is precisely the ingredient for radical thought!

The Inverse Square Law of Conversations

February 2010

All of us are probably familiar with people who command attention in group conversations, and we're all familiar with those who shy away from the spotlight. In a business meeting, it's quite common to hear the same loud opinion voiced in many different ways before you get a glimpse of the quiet opinion. We likely belong to one of these two categories ourselves.

The Inverse Square Law of Conversations is a tactical tool to help manage these two extremes in group situations like meetings.

The law says that the amount of attention one deserves is inversely proportional to the amount of attention one commands.

When following this law, one needs to take greater efforts to uncover opinions from the quiet and subdued. One also needs to recognize that the loud and outspoken need no such effort and should actually be ignored every so often. At the same time, be sure not to pass judgment on the quality of the comments made by either type – just be mindful that you're more likely to hear loud comments and miss the quiet ones.

I should mention a few considerations when practicing this law.

First, the outspoken will express their views even in the face of controversy, while those who avoid attention usually need the group to support their opinions before they feel comfortable enough to express them. This is certainly a generalization, but true in many situations. The idea is that it's more acceptable to attack the opinions of the outspoken than those of the withdrawn. Be careful to express judgment depending on the individual.

The final consideration is that the outspoken must either refrain from serving as the chair of conversations or adopt a quiet demeanor when serving as chair. For example, the chair should strive to provide as much airtime for each of the opinions in the room.

It's also probably wise for the chair to hold their personal opinion silent until it needs to be revealed. And when the chair seeks each person's conclusion at the end of the meeting, they should avoid going around the room in a circle. Instead, it's better they seek the quiet opinions before they get to the outspoken ones.

Much of this probably seems like common sense, but the point is to intentionally consider this law every time you're in a meeting.

You'll find yourself behaving differently, both in how you express your opinions and how you receive others'.

The Power of Electronic Conversations

June 2014

Many articles have been written about the shortcomings of electronic communication and how it's negatively affecting face-to-face communication. We are all aware of how telephone calls and personal visits have been substituted by text messages and emails. Many loathe the trend, while others have embraced it. Most will admit that, while electronic communication provides convenience and speed, it lacks the bandwidth of a face-to-face conversation where the nuances of voice, intonation and gesture add so much value.

While I admit that there are drawbacks to electronic communication, I want to highlight an underrated benefit.

But first, let me give you some context. Over several months now, employees of LogiStyle have been working closely with employees of another company situated in a different city as a result of our pending merger. Each of the two companies has enjoyed the luxury of having its employees located in one facility, in one town. And both companies have fostered an empowered organization where employees rely on close personal communication with each other. When you had a question or a difference of opinion, you walked over to someone's office or had a corridor conversation. Now that people are working across time zones, communication is not as easy.

Let's look at a scenario. Let's say a manager needs to make an important decision and there are five people who can give significant input. The manager knows their initial positions are likely to differ, so she explores two methods to effectively gather their input. She can either visit each of the five individuals one-on-one to gather their input or call a meeting with all of them to have a collective conversation. Clearly, if she opts for one-on-one communication, she can react to the emotions of each individual and be more tactful in making them feel that they are being heard. But if she chooses that option, would the input of each individual have the benefit of other points of view? And would everybody in that group be convinced that everybody else heard the same arguments?

In keeping with the nature of this blog, my stance is logically provocative: **collective conversations create value while collections of individual, two-way conversations destroy value.**

Here's another example. A corporation's by-laws usually call for a majority of directors on the board to vote for passing a resolution. And these by-laws usually allow for the board, in place of a meeting, to pass resolutions by unanimous written consent, wherein each director consents without a collective conversation. Why do they allow majority to rule in collective conversations but require unanimity when the conversation is not collective? For the very reason described above: when the conversation isn't collective, a variety of viewpoints cannot enrich the judgment of each individual.

Now let's return to the topic of electronic communication.

When groups, teams, projects and companies become larger and more geographically dispersed, collective conversations become more difficult. Even arranging a conference call becomes tedious. The result is multiple two-way individual conversations, often partitioned based on their location. You lose the value that comes out of collective conversations and inherit the costs of partitioned conversations.

How can we avoid this? Electronic conversations!

Electronic conversations provide the modern equivalent of a village square. When a difficult topic needs to be discussed, start the conversation electronically and let people chime in collectively, allowing them to express and rebut different points of view. Use it as the village square before you walk into town hall. But remember, don't allow people to mingle too long in the village square. You have to strike a balance. Too much back and forth electronic conversation will quickly degenerate into emotional debate and regurgitation. Force people to express their positions in terms of facts and interpretations – facts that can be verified and interpretations that describe what they conclude from those facts. Close the electronic conversation with a conference call so you can have a live, collective conversation.

No doubt electronic communication has its weaknesses, and one-on-one conversations have their advantages.

But one-on-one conversations are not always better. They can actually be detrimental to the organization as a whole. It can create miscommunication and division within the organization. And as an organization continues to grow, it would be wise to remember the underappreciated and unifying power of electronic collective conversations.

Do You Tweet?

November 2013

Many years ago, when most of us had begun to use automated teller machines around the world, my elderly father-in-law brought a significant amount of cash with him while visiting my wife and me in Portland, Oregon. His reasoning was that since his little bank in Boston did not have branches in my city, he could not use his ATM card. That incident reminded me of the story – possibly an urban myth – about the man who went to his bank every day to withdraw and count his money to ensure that the bank still had it.

Eventually, new technologies and ways of thinking make the previous generation feel somewhat left out.

How many of you have children in college that never answer their cellphones or respond to your email but will text you back instantaneously? How many of you still use Outlook instead of social media as your primary communication tool? And how many of you have Twitter accounts and tweet on a daily basis?

Some of you probably do, but the rest of us should probably ask ourselves which, when and how new technologies will move past us and leave us behind? The more cognizant we are of this, the more likely we are to stay current. It's easy to dismiss many of the new technologies: "Why do I need to be connected all the time? What do you actually get out of using Facebook? It's just a big waste of time. I don't want to know what somebody is cooking for dinner!"

Keep in mind, these new technologies create new social behaviors that will become tomorrow's social order.

While you're still watching TV created by networks and broadcast by cable or satellite, legions of young people choose to watch their programming exclusively through streaming services like Netflix. Many of them don't even own a TV, yet they watch as much TV or more than you do! If you have never heard of companies like Uber or Lyft, one day you might find your go-to taxi service is out of business and you need an app to "call" a cab. If you are still doing electronic banking on your computer and carrying cash, you might one day find yourself in the same situation as the man who went to the bank every day.

So, what can you do about it?

A few years back I wrote an article titled, *Mentoring from Below* (See page 181), in which I suggested my readers adopt a young person as a mentor to help them embrace and adapt to new technologies. Consider picking one new technology you're unfamiliar with and adopt it, even if it is just for the experience.

Before you accuse me of not practicing what I preach, let me say I took my own advice. I decided to start tweeting.

But like you, I felt that I neither had the time nor the desire to tell others what I was having for dinner. Instead, I decided that I would tweet an extension of my conversations on leadership. With all the travel I do, I often find myself at a leisurely dinner alone at the bar, so I created a Twitter account called Balaji's Dinner Talk. You are welcome to subscribe to it by following me @BalajiAtDinner. My intent is to experience the process but, at the same time, further my conversations on #leadership. I hope you'll join in on those conversations.

Mentoring from Below

November 2008

Recently, LogiStyle offered a scholarship at a human resources conference. It was meant to promote innovative thinking in creating intentional corporate cultures. Credit for this month's topic goes to Toni Jaffe, the winner of that scholarship.

Toni's idea is to promote mentoring from below, and I'd like to elaborate on that idea. Toni suggests that in addition to traditional mentoring, where experienced stalwarts mentor young upstarts, we should promote the idea of vibrant, progressive young people mentoring the stuck-in-the-mud older generation. (Rest assured, Toni put it far more politely.)

But is there merit to the idea? Well, how many CEOs and senior level executives use modern technology beyond basic office automation, email, voicemail and possibly text messaging? Isn't there an opportunity for senior executives to establish direct interactions with their large staff through internal blogs? Do you see many of them use RSS feeds to stay up to date with their markets, customers and the like? Are they familiar with modern forms of community interaction, as modeled by Flickr, Prosper, Pandora or others that might change the model of commerce in the future? And if some of this doesn't mean much to you, Toni might well rest her case.

Toni suggests that senior executives adopt a young upstart in their company as their technology mentor. The executive can return the favor by mentoring them in business.

Both parties could benefit from this unusual two-way mentoring from below. The purpose is not just to educate the executives on newer technologies. A partnership between a seasoned executive and a progressive upstart can give rise to business ideas that are shaped by experience and poised for the future.

Employ Your Candidates Before You Hire Them

November 2009

We recently hired a new marketing assistant, and in the hiring process, we were pleasantly surprised at the breadth and depth of candidates that were available in this economy. Nonetheless, it was a daunting task to weed through more than a hundred applications and select the best candidate. Having narrowed it down to a short list through phone interviews, we chose to use a technique that we thought was befitting our brand. That is, we thought it was provocatively logical – not to mention worthy fodder for a *Food for Thought* article!

We decided to hire (as in pay) each of the shortlisted candidates to do the same task – one that can be accomplished without much knowledge of the company's internal affairs.

In our case, it had something to do with our website. The idea was to focus the interviewing process on how they go about doing that job and, in the process, how they interact with the people in the company. Lest visions of *The Apprentice* enter your mind, I am not suggesting a mean-spirited, face-to-face competition but rather a chance to evaluate the work of each of the candidates.

Our experience was very informative!

We saw how they think, how they question status quo, how they ask for clarification when needed and make independent assumptions when appropriate. We saw what process they used to get the job done and how they evaluate their own work. And all of this happened in a real environment with real issues pertinent to our company. We found ourselves hiring based on how they performed rather than on what they told us of their performance. The reason we insisted on payment (albeit not quite at market rates) is to instill an obligation on their part. Needless to say, the task you choose for them is critical to the success of the exercise.

Although at first it may seem like an expensive way to find the right candidate, consider how worthwhile it is to find the right person and how expensive replacing the wrong one can be.

Do Your Meetings Drag On? Try This!

April 2008

Meetings: they're unavoidable. But you want to be sure you're getting value for your time. This month's *Food for Thought* is a bit light-hearted – so much so that you might wonder (given the date) whether I'm serious – but trust me. It maintains my brand of being provocatively logical.

I offer three ideas for keeping meetings crisp and short.

The first, now practiced by many, is to hold standing meetings. You could go to the extreme and enforce standing meetings by removing every chair from your conference rooms.

The second idea, likely to be new and provocative, is to institute a buzzer in conference rooms that goes off every ten minutes or so. Protocol would require that, at the sound of the buzzer, all participants stand and observe ten seconds of silence. During that silence, participants think about how relevant the current conversation is to the meeting's agenda. At the end of the silence, participants resume their discussion, regularly questioning any unnecessary detours.

The third idea is not only provocative, but also quite intrusive. Hand out play money to all participants in a meeting. Participants are then expected to drop a predetermined amount of money – say $20 every ten minutes – into a bowl, representing the cost of their time. The meeting chair then draws the money from the bowl and sees what value the meeting should have created. This approach makes you constantly focus on the value of your meetings.

These ideas are fun, if not dramatic, but their real value is in making you think more intentionally about your meetings. And when you think about it, do you ever want to be in a meeting that's not intentional?

Don't Discount; Give It Away for FREE!

August 2011

I've had executive experience with product-based businesses and service-based businesses, and in both cases, customers and clients seek special discounts. They feel they're getting a deal when they land a discount. Vendors often tend to price accordingly, recognizing that the net price is going to be discounted from its listed price. Published discounts available to all parties, with rules and restrictions, are certainly understandable. For example, at LogiStyle we offer early registration discounts encouraging people to register early for our workshops. We incentivize them to register early, giving us some assurance that seats will be filled. Similarly, product-based companies often offer volume discounts, recognizing that they enjoy economies of scale.

How about offering special discounts when a customer or client is on the fence?

Is there any business rationale for entertaining such special discounts? If so, who gets it and who doesn't? Do the loud and obnoxious or the adamant and stubborn get these discounts, leaving the rule-abiding and cooperative customer paying list price? Will the practice of offering special discounts cause more people to line up for them? Once you start offering them, can you really say, "Sorry, we don't offer special discounts," when you change your mind?

Considering this, I'd like to offer a provocative solution.

Adopt a policy of no special discounts with the caveat that, when you feel compelled, you'll give it away for free.

At LogiStyle we make a practice of not offering any special discounts beyond our published ones. However, on occasion, when we have a potential client who has not been exposed to our workshops and presents an opportunity for a large volume of business, we *have* extended a complimentary invitation.

The advantage of offering something for free instead of offering a discount is that the client or customer is much less likely to ask for another unit for free.

They appreciate that the business cannot keep giving things away for free. When you give them a special discount, on the other hand, they will want that discount the next time around.

You might think that this technique works for service-based, but not product-based, industries.

Not true! I'd like to share an experience I had with a high-tech company that worked out very well. Industrial customers of high-tech products fully comprehend that there is a manufacturing cost for hardware, but they often feel they should get software either free or heavily discounted. At this high-tech company, we did things quite differently. We had a strict rule of not discounting software. So we would give away hardware for free but refused to discount software. This way, the customer never dared to ask for another free unit of hardware and understood the software wouldn't be discounted.

The game of individual discounting is a slippery slope. It might feel good to close a deal by offering a small discount and getting a piece of profitable business in return. You might feel that between the time saved and the business closed, you have come out ahead. However, I'd argue you're simply adding a long-term liability to your balance sheet to give your income statement a temporary boost.

On the Ethics of Referral Marketing and Group Marketing

May 2011

Many companies offer their clients an incentive when a referral results in new business. In that situation, does the client have an obligation to disclose that transaction to the friend they referred? Does the company have an obligation to ensure such transparency? These questions become more pertinent the bigger the incentive is. Referral marketing is fraught with these ethical issues. At LogiStyle, where all of our business comes from word of mouth referrals, I have often thought of offering incentives. But we've refrained from doing so because we'd first like to find good answers to these important questions.

Group marketing recently became popular with successes like Groupon gaining major press and attention from Google.

The original concept of group marketing was to encourage customers to use their social and professional network to amass a large enough interest in a commercial offer to make the offer economically viable for the sponsoring company. Group marketing provides goods and services at a discounted price to all members of a group provided the group is adequately large. The group members are then encouraged to promote the sponsoring company and the associated offer to their network of friends and recruit more members into the group. In short, the more you generate interest in a product among your friends, the more deals you and your friends get to enjoy. Here, the transaction is transparent and all members of the group benefit from it. The ethical questions of referral marketing do not apply to group marketing. Groupon, originally focused on retail customers of B2C companies, grew so popular that they transformed their business model from requiring a minimum group size to limiting the size of the group.

The concept of group marketing is equally applicable to B2B companies like LogiStyle.

However, no clear leader has emerged offering group marketing services to B2B companies. The reason for this could be one doesn't need an established clearinghouse for group marketing to B2B clients. Now let's explore how a B2B company, like LogiStyle, might be able to use group marketing in some provocative ways. The strategy of group marketing is to invite your clients to promote your products and services to their networks by offering an attractive discount to the entire group if the group is large enough.

LogiStyle is in the business of offering workshops to corporate executives.

Workshops are scheduled speculatively in a specific city and marketed to clients in the area. Clearly, the business model requires a minimum number of clients to sign up for the workshop for LogiStyle to break even, and the profits stem from the incremental clients that sign up beyond the minimum. There might be some parallels between LogiStyle's business model and yours. Perhaps B2B group marketing is in both our futures.

We have considered incentivizing our clients to promote our workshops by offering a discount to the first X number of registrants to a workshop, provided X number of registrants actually sign up.

The client is given an incentive to promote our workshop, amass the required number of registrants and secure their discount. But what if we were to offer a discount to all members of a group with the discount being proportional to the size of the group? In other words, if you can amass a larger group, you and your friends will all enjoy a larger discount. We are still toying with this idea. Or even more provocatively, what if we combined the concepts of group marketing with the older concept of pyramid marketing? Will we be bumping up against the ethical questions of referral marketing, with which we started this *Food for Thought?*

Group marketing is just one way businesses are adapting to new technologies and changing tastes. What other changes to the marketplace might apply to your business? Even a brief mental exercise like this one could lead to big changes and opportunities for your company down the line. I hope these thoughts cause you to think about the relevance of this new concept of B2B group marketing to your own business.

Service Departments Understand Customers' Concern

March 2010

As a leader in your company, how much personal time do you spend with the people in your sales and marketing departments? How about your product development people? Manufacturing employees? How much time do you spend with the people in the service and support departments? If you are like most CEOs, chances are you're more in touch with sales than you are with the service guy. Why is that?

After all, the people in the service and support departments of your company are probably closest to your customers, particularly those customers with a concern about your products and services. Yes, your sales department probably understands why customers buy what you offer, but the service and support department is much more in tune with how happy they are after the purchase.

As a leader in your company, particularly as the CEO or division president, how often do you get direct input from those departments to find out where your offerings are lacking and how to improve them?

CEOs should periodically take a morning out of their busy schedules, walk over to their call center, put on a headset and listen in on the incoming calls. The CEO need not, and should not, be a participant in the call – only a silent observer. There is no better way to learn what customers are saying, how your front line is staving off irate customers and where in your product lines you need to make some changes.

Bill Kabele, who has served as a general manager for a variety of companies, always made a practice of visiting the service department when he visited his remote sites – particularly foreign sites. His rationale was that the service manager would tell you things that you might not otherwise hear because intermediate management filters that information. He would point out that returned units sitting on service department shelves tell the tale of a customer's woes far better than any management report ever could.

Whatever the nature of your business, start thinking more about the state of your service and support departments.

How can you get direct input from these front line personnel? Consider inviting a few of these front line people into your strategic planning meeting. Have your product designers spend a day in the service or support department. It's easy to recognize individuals in your service or support departments by nominating them for an award. But there is no better recognition – of the entire department – than to spend a morning learning from one of them.

A Spoonful of My Own Medicine

August 2014

This article is a personal message from me to you. The backdrop is our recently announced merger. I want to express my own intentions in light of the merger and, motivated by that, ask you some provocative questions. Last month, we announced that LogiStyle has merged with a Winnipeg, Manitoba based advertising company called Think Shift. Together, we intend to help our clients create intentional brands, intentional cultures and intentional strategies based on a foundation of intentional leadership.

We are combining Think Shift's promise of releasing the potential in brands, organizations and people, with LogiStyle's promise of intentionality to create our own concept of Potentionality.

At the outset, I want to reassure our clients that I am not retiring or bowing out. On the contrary, this merger is intended to allow me to spend more time creating and delivering content. I will serve as the operating chairman of the combined company, which will be called Think Shift, and David Baker, the current CEO of Think Shift, will serve as the CEO of the combined company. Both David and I will be spending a lot of time with clients, delivering content.

Now, modesty aside, I am a pretty intentional guy. So if this isn't an exit strategy, why would I enter into such a merger?

I want to tell you a story that will hopefully inspire you to think of your own story. When I left Planar, my last employer in corporate America, I had a body of material that I had developed for more than 30 years, and I decided to commercialize it by offering workshops for corporate executives. My thinking was that I would build LogiStyle into a viable business that I could, at the right time, take into retirement, throttling my involvement as I wished. I wasn't concerned that LogiStyle provided neither financial leverage nor financial equity. I was content for it to be a one-man show – supported by a young staff that I groomed. I was largely motivated by the passion I had rather than the wealth it generated.

Many of you are aware of my definition of Leadership: Leverage + Legacy.

Hearing my pitch on becoming an intentional leader, David Baker came to my **L³ Legacy program** and wrote his **Leadership Agenda**. His experience was transformative, not only for himself but for his company – financially, culturally and strategically – as he put each member of his leadership team through the program. He was so convinced by the approach, he signed up to the graduate-level program called **Beyond L³**, where we focus on the "why" of your Leadership Agenda.

It was during the three days of that program that he forced me to reconcile my plans for LogiStyle with my own "why" of my Leadership Agenda. If my Inspired Imperatives (a concept discussed in the Beyond L³ program) cause me to desire high leverage and long legacy, why am I settling for the sunset strategy of LogiStyle?

He invited me to come visit him in Winnipeg to witness the impact I'd had on him and his company.

Lo and behold, I was floored. This advertising company had combined my concepts of intentional leadership and intentional culture with their own concepts of intentional brand, using their prowess of communication and storytelling to bring much of my material to life. But there was more! Not only had they fully internalized the material, they were teaching it to each other and to their clients. They had gone beyond absorbing my material – they enhanced and promulgated it. I asked myself, "Is this not leverage? Is this not legacy?"

Long story short, we concluded that combining forces would further both our goals.

We spent a year providing our combined services to multiple clients and the marriage was cemented. Last month, our companies merged. We intend to provide a broader set of services and offerings to our combined set of clients and we look forward to talking to you more about our plans.

Now why is this relevant to you?

I want to inspire you to articulate your own story and then question it. Tell your story. What are your plans for your company, for your career? I suspect you have made some definite plans for what you want to accomplish and for the people who will succeed you. Those plans are probably based on certain assumptions – assumptions about what you consider possible, what you consider unlikely, what you would want and what you think is undesirable, etc. Question those assumptions. For each assumption you question, explore how your current plan would change. Then construct the most plausible alternative scenario for your story that invalidates a few of your assumptions. Tell the story of that alternative scenario. Give it a taste. You might find it palatable. You may even find it enticing. I did.

Thank you to our clients and well-wishers for all the success we have had to date and the future it has offered our company. I am excited to expand the delivery of my content and approach, including these *Food for Thought* articles, which will be delivered under our new company name, Think Shift.

Caution: Consultant Ahead

October 2012

This topic is on the use of consultants. On a side note, I should say that, because I enjoy being provocative and controversial, I always run the risk of having someone take my advice personally. That is not my intent. Like my blog's title suggests, my comments should be taken as food for thought, not as a comment on anyone in particular. Are we good? Great!

I should say up front, I am wary of consultants – particularly those whose deliverables are elusive, whose quality of results is subjective and whose effectiveness is immeasurable.

Let's start with an old question that's become cliché: Do consultants simply borrow your watch to tell you the time? Consultants come in varied types, providing a variety of services. I'd like to offer classifications for three types of consultants.

The first type is Talent for Rent.

You need a specific talent – a web designer to build your web pages, a lawyer to write a contract, an accountant to prepare your taxes, etc. Your choice is to hire or rent. This is purely a financial decision. You decide that you don't have long-term needs for this talent – or enough need to hire a full-time person – so you decide to rent the services on a fee-for-service basis. Typically, these are very specialized skills. The talent for rent serves you a product (a web page designed, a contract prepared, tax papers filed) that is usually mostly objective. Again, the decision to hire these consultants is purely a financial decision between hiring and renting.

The second type of consultant is a Teacher – essentially a walking, talking book.

This is someone who has extensive knowledge on a specific subject. You hire them to give a talk, a course, a seminar, a workshop, etc., so that you can get a lively experience of that book. The book, whether written or unwritten, does not change based on the audience. The consultant might choose to focus on specific chapters in their book based on your needs, but the pages of the book were already written before they walked into your facility.

Examples include a project management course, a safety seminar or a leadership workshop. Since they know the book in great detail, and since they have infinite capacity to pull information from that book, they can answer questions on the spot. But they are merely reading from their own book. The decision to hire such a consultant is essentially a decision to buy a live performance of the book.

The third type of consultant is an Advisor – someone who studies your situation and gives you advice on what you should do.

The assumption is that, even though you and your colleagues have an in-depth understanding of your situation and have examined the issues in great detail over a long period of time, this consultant can walk in, examine your situation over a shorter period of time and provide you with advice that you might not have considered.

The premise with these consultants is that their advice is useful for one of two reasons. First, even though their understanding of the situation is probably shallower than yours, their breadth of knowledge and experience allows them to come up with ideas, suggestions and solutions you've never thought of. Second, because you are so close to the situation, you might not entertain certain solutions that are more obvious to an outsider. I question that first premise and have some alternatives to the second.

I question whether, in most realistic business situations (which are usually quite complex and deeply constrained), an outside consultant can gain enough of an understanding to offer you advice more meaningful than you can.

The question is, will the consultant's breadth of experience and depth of knowledge be so vast that it will compensate for their shallower understanding of your situation? How about the advantage of their outside perspective? We agree that an outsider will have a perspective that might be overlooked by the insider, but there are other ways of making yourself more open to out-of-the-box thinking that would help you in the long run. By developing the ability to constantly question why you do things the way you do (or think the way you do), you and your organization can create a long-term solution. You can gain that outsider perspective and avoid hiring a consultant to provide that perspective on an individual basis.

Another problem I have with the "advisor" consultant is that the quality of their advice is often difficult to quantify and they get paid before the results can be measured.

So if you choose to hire such a consultant, I suggest that you compare the cost of their advice against the cost of a guarantee. Understand how much it would cost to get the advice you are seeking. Ask the consultant how you could measure the results of their advice should you choose to implement it. Then ask the consultant how much risk premium they would need to charge if the payment were contingent upon achieving those results. Their response will help you see how confident they are in their own advice. With that information, you can choose to hire the consultant on a fee-for-service basis, on a contingent payment upon deliverables basis, or not hire them at all.

I have explored similar models for the workshops I offer.

What if I offered people the option of paying for the workshop after they attend it, based on their satisfaction? To be fair to the people who pay up front, those who pay later would have to understand that a premium applies if they're satisfied with the workshop and all can benefit from the confidence shown by the offer.

CPSIA information can be obtained
at www.ICGtesting.com
Printed in the USA
FSOW04n1839090216
16755FS